PRAISE

"*Leap* addresses a fundamental question so many women face today: How do I architect my career to find fulfillment and avoid emotional burnout? A must-read for working women and parents, whether you need inspiration to take the leap or simply comfort to know that you are not alone."

—Eve Rodsky, *New York Times* best-selling author of *Fair Play* and *Find Your Unicorn Space*

"*Leap* is a breath of fresh air for women who feel lost or disillusioned as they navigate their careers (and broader lives) in today's world. The real-life stories are honest and relatable. The guided reflections are pragmatic and actionable. A valuable read for any woman at a crossroads in her career!"

—Lauren McGoodwin, founder and CEO of Career Contessa and best-selling author of *Power Moves: How Women Can Pivot, Reboot, and Build a Career of Purpose*

"*Leap* is full of encouraging case studies from courageous women navigating career changes large and small. Their stories, mixed with Jess's helpful insights on challenges unique to women, will help you forge your *own* path forward—one that resonates with who you are at your most authentic core, not who you *should* be to please others. It's time to take the reins and thrive, not just survive. *Leap* is a light to guide the way."

—Jenny Blake, podcaster and author of *Free Time*, *Pivot*, and *Life after College*

"If you are staring at your career and wondering, *Is this it?*, Jess has an answer: *No!* Packed with relatable examples and practical self-reflection exercises, *Leap* isn't just for women; it's for anyone seeking greater clarity, confidence, and control over their careers."

—Gorick Ng, *Wall Street Journal* best-selling author of *The Unspoken Rules*

"After fifteen long years working in four Fortune 100 companies, I came to the conclusion that the workplace isn't working for women of all kinds, especially women from underrepresented groups, and especially women with children. Now more than ever, women need real, sustainable pathways to achieving the life they've always dreamed of—a life full of hope and possibilities, one they can achieve only when they take bold and audacious steps and, with Jess's step-by-step guide, leap forward. This book is relevant also for employers who value the contributions of women and strive to retain them."

—Blessing Adesiyan, founder and CEO of MH WorkLife

"Jess Galica's voice is a must-hear for career-driven women. Her book, *Leap*, empowers us to own and revise our career narratives. Through a compelling mix of stories and data, Jess illustrates that we already possess the tools for major career transformations—all we lack is the impetus. Consider *Leap* your necessary nudge to make that leap and confidently bet on yourself."

—Laurie Ruettimann, author of *Betting on You*

"Thank you to Jess Galica for helping us get out of the starting blocks! As a woman who took a major pivot later in my career, I wish I had had *Leap* years ago. I love the advice 'You know more than you are telling yourself.' It's up to us to continue to reevaluate our career trajectory and ensure that we are doing work that energizes us."

—Ellen Bailey, vice president of business and culture transformation at Harvard Business Publishing and owner of the Bailey Difference

"If you are a woman questioning your career path, feeling overwhelmed or dissatisfied with work, or unsure about your next steps, you need this book! Change takes self-reflection and courage, and *Leap* will give you the inspiration and guidance to take action on creating your best life. Emotions are a major part of any transformation, and Galica addresses the impact of feelings head-on in the book, encouraging readers to both acknowledge and honor what arises. Filled with relatable and empowering career stories, *Leap* takes you on a journey that will leave you changed and ready to embark on a path to greater fulfillment."

—Dawn Graham, author of *Switchers: How Smart Professionals Change Careers*

"When it comes to women and career change, Jess Galica is the expert you need to follow. Her expertise covers the topics that matter most today for women navigating corporate careers. *Leap* is packed with inspiring stories from real women about building a successful career, the twists and turns they navigate, and the obstacles they overcome to find success and fulfillment at work. *Leap* also arms readers with pragmatic exercises and the know-how to make real and lasting change. A must-read for any woman rethinking her career."

—Andrea Simon, PhD, CEO of Simon Associates Management Consultants and author of *Rethink* and *On the Brink*

"Jessica Galica, in her book *Leap*, adds a new dimension to the career literature/self-help books that are out there by focusing on women and the unique challenges they face as they navigate careers in these complex and modern times. In the first part of the book, she organizes the chapters around the major emotions that women experience, which can be catalysts for driving their career change. Through her storytelling, her reflection exercises, and her recommended strategies, she acknowledges that women are so much more than titles, skills, and competencies. She acknowledges that women are complex beings with many roles and responsibilities and that they need to honor their emotions to know when change is needed, so that they can show up as healthy and fully aligned human beings in any work they choose to do. This book gives women the permission to lean into their emotions to find what is authentically right in the next step in their career journeys."

—Gayle Grader, director of executive career development at MIT Sloan School of Management

LEAP

**WHY IT'S TIME TO
LET GO TO
GET AHEAD
IN YOUR CAREER**

LEAP

JESSICA GALICA

FC
FAST
COMPANY
Press

I hope Leap inspires you in exactly the way you need!

This publication is designed to provide accurate and authoritative information in regard to the subject matter covered. It is sold with the understanding that the publisher and author are not engaged in rendering legal, accounting, or other professional services. Nothing herein shall create an attorney-client relationship, and nothing herein shall constitute legal advice or a solicitation to offer legal advice. If legal advice or other expert assistance is required, the services of a competent professional should be sought.

Fast Company Press
New York, New York
www.fastcompanypress.com

Copyright © 2023 Jessica Galica

All rights reserved.

Thank you for purchasing an authorized edition of this book and for complying with copyright law. No part of this book may be reproduced, stored in a retrieval system, or transmitted by any means, electronic, mechanical, photocopying, recording, or otherwise, without written permission from the copyright holder.

This work is being published under the Fast Company Press imprint by an exclusive arrangement with Fast Company. Fast Company and the Fast Company logo are registered trademarks of Mansueto Ventures, LLC. The Fast Company Press logo is a wholly owned trademark of Mansueto Ventures, LLC.

Distributed by River Grove Books

Design and composition by Greenleaf Book Group and Mimi Bark
Cover design by Greenleaf Book Group and Mimi Bark
Cover image used under license from ©Shutterstock.com/Leremy; ©Shutterstock.com/Korrapon Karapan

Publisher's Cataloging-in-Publication data is available.

Print ISBN: 978-1-63908-055-7

eBook ISBN: 978-1-63908-056-4

First Edition

To A. and H.:
May you embrace the journey of writing—
and sometimes rewriting—the story of your life.

To Adanna and Bean:
Thank you for reading and for your friendship.

To Matt:
I love writing our story together.

CONTENTS

INTRODUCTION 1

PART I: Why You Feel This Way 11

   CHAPTER 1: Dissatisfied 13

   CHAPTER 2: Isolated 25

   CHAPTER 3: Guilty 35

   CHAPTER 4: Reluctant 45

   CHAPTER 5: Afraid 59

PART II: How to Embrace 69

   CHAPTER 6: Role Models 71

   CHAPTER 7: New Possibilities 77

   CHAPTER 8: Risks 85

   CHAPTER 9: Your Supporters 91

   CHAPTER 10: The Test-and-Learn Approach 105

   CHAPTER 11: Preparing to Leap 115

   CHAPTER 12: Ready, Set, Go 125

PART III: The Ways You'll Win 133
    CHAPTER 13: Feel Engaged 135
    CHAPTER 14: Be Empowered 147
    CHAPTER 15: Build Resilience 157
CONCLUSION 167
APPENDIX: Reflection Tool Kit 171
NOTES 183
ABOUT THE AUTHOR 197

INTRODUCTION

In 2018, Michelle Obama published her record-shattering memoir, *Becoming*.[1] It was one of the first times that a woman in the public eye pulled back the curtain and gave the world a raw, honest look at a life and woman that seemed infallible. Nothing was off the table. Michelle shared vulnerable moments and admissions—her marriage required counseling, she struggled with infertility, she lost loved ones, and she grew up amid worsening structural racism in her Chicago neighborhood. Women flocked to the book precisely because of this vulnerability. Because, despite being an exceptional woman with an extraordinary trajectory, through all these imperfect stories that Michelle let us into, we also saw ourselves.

I saw myself most in the pages where Michelle talks about her career. Page after page, I found myself whispering out loud, "Exactly—yes, that's exactly how I feel too." We meet Michelle as a little girl with big dreams and a foolproof checklist to achieve them. We see her check every box and climb the ladder—she earns good grades in school; gains admission to Princeton University, followed by Harvard Law School; and finally, lands a coveted job at an elite law firm. Her checklist works. *She's made it*, we think.

LEAP

But then, the floor falls out from under Michelle. She remains perched at the top, in a swanky office, driving a nice car, wearing nice clothes, and earning a generous paycheck. But she starts to realize that the view from the top is, well, just not that great. Michelle is unfulfilled. She is purposeless. She is exhausted. At the same time, she wants more. She is wasting her potential. How can this possibly make sense? And how can she complain about a job this good? Michelle feels selfish. She is ashamed. She worries what others will think.

I am right there with her. I grab the book tighter. Because I see her. And I see myself.

IT IS NOW 2023, and working women have reached a collective crisis. The far-reaching effects of the COVID-19 pandemic have exacerbated the already-daunting challenges and trade-offs that women face in their professional lives. The result is a devastating impact on women's work advancement. Startingly, in the United States alone, more than three million women left the workforce during the pandemic, and a staggering one-third of working mothers left their jobs, reduced their hours, or expressed intentions to leave. Only a meager one in five women feel empowered at work to ignore nonessential demands that encroach on their lives beyond traditional working hours.[2] Working mothers are so burned out that they are resorting to communal gatherings to let out primal screams. Yes, you heard that right—gathering to simply scream together in frustration. But women know the dirtier secret: The primal screams of women and mothers is not just a pandemic problem. This is a crisis long in the making.

Even before the pandemic, more than half of US workers expressed unhappiness with their jobs. Across the world, only 15 percent of full-time employees report feeling engaged with—involved and enthusiastic about—their work.[3] One consequence is a perpetual cycle of job changing, as employees jump from one job to another to find something tolerable enough that it sticks. On average, we transition through twelve

Introduction

jobs throughout the prime of our career. If you're an average millennial, you will change jobs four times within the first decade of your career.[4] The list of statistics goes on. But long story short? An increasing number of people are struggling to find their career identity and formulate a long-term career vision. They are unwittingly signing up for two- or three-year career sprints but never training, or even contemplating signing up, for the career marathon that lies ahead.

Finding fulfillment in the modern career path is complex for everyone, but it's even more complex for women. Corporate women feel gaslighted. Women—especially millennial women—grew up with powerful narratives telling them they could have it all in career and in life. They heard messages like "Break the glass ceiling," "Lean in," and "You can have it all." So we put our heads down and did everything "right." But now that we are picking up our heads, we are wondering, *How did we get here?*

As women, we've built our careers on these narratives. But the problem is, those stories were never built for us. After leaning in and chipping away at the glass ceiling, women in the workforce are exasperated. They are dissatisfied. They are unfulfilled. They are exhausted. Today women resonate with different narratives: "It's a concrete ceiling after all," "You can never have it all," and "Lean out, opt out—or more accurately, be pushed out."

Women need new narratives, now more than ever. Against the backdrop of recovery from a global pandemic, the rise of the Great Resignation, and the impact of the Shecession, there has never been a time when more women are redefining what a successful career looks like and recalibrating how to build it. When it comes to women and work, it is a time of unprecedented reinvention. Today's generation of women is the first to believe that there is more to work than putting their heads down to get ahead in a corporate world that was designed for men. We are gradually awakening to the idea that maybe there's a way to do things differently. We are giving ourselves permission to play by different rules. We are unlocking what we've always had the capacity to do: break free from traditional narratives of success to start writing our own stories.

Reinvention requires change. On the one hand, changing or reinventing one's career is nothing new. Today we generally accept that career pivots are the new normal—after all, you are likely to have twelve or more jobs in your career. That's a lot of change. It is no longer realistic to envision our careers as a straight path where we predictably climb one ladder rung after another. The modern career path is less like a ladder and more like a river. Today's careers meander. They are influenced by the environment around us—the people we meet along the way, the bad weather that surprises us—and we cannot always see what is around the corner. Most of us acknowledge that career reinvention is no longer a choice. It is a necessity. That's why we see plenty of books about this new behavior—*Pivot*, or *Switchers*, or *When to Jump*—helping people understand how to pivot, switch, or leave their career. But I have an important question: Why isn't anyone talking about career reinvention specifically for women?

The reality is clear: Gender informs every step of career reinvention—from why, to when, to how. Today's unprecedented need for career reinvention is not just a problem; it is a *women's* problem. Both third-party research and my own interviews with women show us why career changing is unique for women: Women want to reinvent their careers for different reasons than men do. Women feel isolated in male-dominated corporate environments that are not designed for them. Mothers face the heavy task of balancing work and a disproportionate amount of household labor and childcare. Women know they can make a unique contribution but lose confidence because they are in the wrong arena. Women are drawn to more purposeful work that affects their communities. Or they simply have a strong intuition whispering to them, *This isn't it*.

- *Why:* The same things repeatedly hold women back from career change. Women want to avoid risk. They are afraid of failure. Or

Introduction

they feel guilty for wanting more. They do not want to fail feminism by stepping aside, stepping off, or stepping back from an established track. Women are so focused on meeting the needs of others that they lose touch with their own needs—they literally *don't know what they want* in their career.

- *When:* Timing matters. Women hold off on career changes because they have been conditioned by corporate environments to lack confidence. Women are forced to prepare more than men to get the same results, thanks to gender biases in hiring, promotions, and investment. And women factor into career decisions timing around motherhood and family far more frequently than their male counterparts. In fact, many women reinvent their career specifically to align with the needs of their family.

- *How:* With limited women in leadership positions, women must rely on alternative support systems and like-minded communities that provide access to information and networks. They diligently, painstakingly prepare because they know they must overcome bias and discrimination, especially for women of color. Even when highly prepared, women rely on supporters to close confidence gaps. And they often build side hustles before making a major leap.

Women face significant complexity when they decide to shift their career path. Women are building their careers against the backdrop of recovery from a global pandemic, which introduces a disproportionate level of chaos and complexity for women to navigate. Beyond the pandemic, today's careers simply come with new challenges. Careers used to be like ladders—predictable, linear, singular. But today's careers are fluid, with twists and turns, always changing and evolving. And in the face of this complexity, pivots are challenging. However, when women pivot, they also earn incredible rewards. A career change gives women the immediate benefit of a new job. But more than that, women achieve a valuable mindset shift: they see what is possible when they ditch traditional career expectations and start playing by their own rules. Women learn to embrace fear, take risks with imperfect information, and be more fearless and empowered. They learn to believe, often for the first time in their career, that they are truly in the driver's seat.[5] They stop believing that their career is happening *to them*. Instead, they believe *they* are making their career happen *for them*. That empowerment makes women more fulfilled. When women take their career and align it with what they want, they are happier and more engaged. They perform better and stay in the race longer.[6] They flow.[7]

Although the art of career reinvention has never been more critical for women, the idea of pivoting your career can be intimidating. In my work with women, I have seen every excuse to not pivot or reinvent a career, such as:

> I don't have the necessary skills to make a change.
>
> I don't want to start over. Starting over feels overwhelming and discouraging.
>
> Expertise is what drives success, so how will I become an expert if I keep changing paths?
>
> I haven't discovered a true calling or sense of purpose.
>
> I don't have a passion.
>
> I can't make money with my passion.
>
> I can't let go of my salary.

All these arguments give women an out to say, "Pivoting is not for me." And while these concerns are valid, in today's workforce, career reinvention is a skill needed to succeed—for everyone. Women who make a career pivot are building the experience needed for ongoing career management and advancement. With each intentional effort and each successful career change, women strengthen their change muscles

Introduction

and develop the habits, behaviors, and mindsets to do it again—and again and again.

I SPENT THE FIRST TEN YEARS of my career ticking off boxes. I followed a checklist, adding more and more gold stars to my resume, to get to the top. During that decade, I jumped into the trending start-up world, completed an MBA at the Massachusetts Institute of Technology (MIT), and worked at a top-tier management consulting firm. With every step, I dutifully checked all the boxes as I climbed the ladder. I was working hard, striving to keep up with my peers, and succumbing to mounting stress. I rarely stopped to pick up my head and look around. Finally, when I did lift my gaze, the consequences of a decade consumed by the pursuit of recognition caught up with me. I woke up and realized that I did not like the career trajectory that lay ahead. I was disengaged from my work. I was unhappy. I felt purposeless. Two profound and persistent questions echoed in my head and in my heart: How did I get here? And why do I feel so empty?

For the first time, I gave myself permission to admit that I had been checking the wrong boxes. I needed a new solution. As a former consultant, I wanted data to understand my options. I began to talk with other women who had asked the same questions I did. I shared what I was feeling with a few close friends and family members and asked, "Do you know of anyone who went through this?" I was inundated with responses. Everyone suggested someone for me to talk to: friends, colleagues, mothers, spouses. The list was endless. And it was overwhelming. I quickly realized that my story—building a career, doing everything "right" but waking up lost—was not unique. This was not a *me* problem. This was a *women* problem.

A few conversations turned into dozens of interviews across three years. I became obsessed with this problem. There were two things to understand: How was this problem affecting women's career trajectories and success? And what were women doing about it? Looking back, I see now that I was also searching for hope—hope that I still had space for a fulfilling career and that I would get unlost enough to find it.

Around the same time, I became pregnant with my daughter. It was transformative. The anticipation of becoming a mom made me look at my career in new ways. Until that point, my career had made up so much of my identity. I knew that was about to change. No matter what career decisions I made, the career slice of the pie was going to become smaller. I was going to make space—more space than I could have ever imagined—for my identity as a mother and caregiver. It was this realization that emboldened me to reinvent myself. I thought, *Do I even have a choice?* Becoming a mom gave me the courage to take the next step with my research and begin writing. Since my daughter became a reality, I have held tight to one powerful wish for her: I want her to be comfortable in her own skin and to be authentically herself. I finally took the same advice and started my journey to transform the way that women experience work. I began building a platform to share career stories and empower all women to write their own career narrative on their own terms. I heard my daughter whispering, "Don't worry about the gold star or what anyone else thinks—go be you."

And just like that, this book was born.

THIS BOOK IS FOR ANYONE who wants women to achieve their highest potential in life. If you are a woman examining your career trajectory or contemplating untapped possibilities, this book will give you inspiration. This is true no matter what stage you are at, whether you are listening for the first time to that voice inside you whispering that there is something more out there or you are already on your journey to executing a career change. You will recognize yourself in the stories, lessons, and emotions shared in the book. If you support a woman career changer in your life—as a manager, spouse, family member, or friend—this book is for you too. It will help you come along for the ride and gain insight into the unique challenges and emotions that

Introduction

women tackle when reinventing their careers. You will see the women in your life in these stories. You may see yourself too.

Though the topic of this book revolves around women and their careers, at its core this is a book about emotions—the emotions that drive our biggest career decisions and how we can harness them to get where we truly want to go. In the first section of the book, each chapter is named for an emotion. I made this choice because all my interviews focused so heavily on the emotional aspect of navigating careers. When interviewing women, I expected the conversations to resemble job interviews—"Tell me about your career history"—as I took notes on the pragmatic tips, tricks, and checklists for women to follow. I was wrong. Instead, the interviews were like therapy sessions or coffee with a trusted friend. When women told me their stories, they talked about what and how they felt: fear, excitement, uncertainty, pain, joy, relief. The common threads were all emotions—the universal feelings, twists, and turns that women experience when figuring out a big career shift.

I want women to feel empowered after reading this book. Each chapter includes reflection exercises that help move women forward. Yet, with each interview I conducted, it became increasingly clear: Women do not need another checklist or another five-step plan. Women are experts at getting things done. What women need, instead, is to be seen. Women want to see narratives and stories about careers that *reflect them*. Storytelling is the most powerful strategy to communicate, teach, and spark change. Research agrees with me that stories, not checklists, are what stick.[8]

You will not only hear from the women I interviewed. Also included are well-known stories of prominent women in leadership today. Sheryl Sandberg's jump to Silicon Valley and how she almost didn't get there. Ava DuVernay's foray into filmmaking after picking up a camera for the first time in her thirties. Ina Garten's impulsive real estate purchase that led to the food empire we know and love today. No matter the woman, I am confident you will feel understanding, empathy, laughter, and joy. You will end up inspired and rooting for every woman on her journey.

Women's experiences are not singular, and this book aims to reflect that. The stories represent women early in their career, women late in their career, women of color, Black women, LGBTQ+ women, mothers, single mothers, and nonparents. However, an important limit is that all stories come from women with experience in *corporate* roles. As a result, there is a level of privilege built into the stories, as a corporate career offers a salaried role, typically with benefits, and with the structure and predictability of a routine corporate schedule. Nearly all the interviewees have the college degrees, and sometimes advanced degrees, necessary to gain access to these corporate roles. Of course, many women lack these privileges. Yet I believe it is beneficial to evaluate women's experiences and gender equity (or lack thereof) in these privileged, corporate environments. If we do not deliver a fair, sustainable, and joyful experience for women in the most privileged careers, we will also not deliver a fair, sustainable, and joyful experience for women employed in less-privileged working environments.

Just as I saw myself in Michelle Obama's story, I hope you see yourself in the stories in this book. I hope the stories remind you that you are not alone. I hope they spark curiosity and inspiration. Most importantly, I hope they empower you to reclaim control and fulfillment in your career. To build a career narrative that reflects *your truth*. To make whatever leap you want to make.

So, what career story will you write?

PART I

WHY YOU FEEL THIS WAY

CHAPTER 1

DISSATISFIED

A LESSON IN WHAT NOT TO DO

I have spent fifteen years building a business career. From one of the world's top global consulting firms to fast-paced tech start-ups, each role has been focused on traditional business work. Advising Fortune 100 companies on corporate strategy and cost reduction. Building partnerships with top global companies like IBM and Deloitte. Quantitative analysis. Business planning. Negotiation. Sales management.

How did I get here?

Growing up, I was a bookworm. By the time I got to college, I chose American studies, a classic liberal arts degree—as far away from my college's business school as you could get—as my major. My thesis explored women and career, how women balancing work and motherhood were depicted in emerging blog and pop culture. I dropped the only business course I took in college: microeconomics. I struggled to understand the content and was disinterested, so I dropped the course halfway through the semester to avoid a poor grade.

LEAP

So how did I end up at MIT, pursuing my MBA at one of the world's top business schools? And then at one of the world's top management consulting firms, knee-deep in Excel models and PowerPoint presentation slides?

Looking back, I can see how. I got to where I am by ignoring my interests and the authentic voice inside my head and heart. Instead, I was guided by the world I saw around me. I looked toward the comfort of commonly climbed career ladders. I asked myself questions such as: What is so-and-so doing? Do people think this job is prestigious? How much money does it pay? This industry seems so competitive and dominated by men, why couldn't I succeed in it too? Is this job as good as the ones my friends are getting?

These drivers were not all bad. They led me to expand my skill set, work at respected and well-run organizations, be trusted with a high level of responsibility, and earn a rewarding salary that made me proud and fulfilled, especially as a woman. But after more than a decade on this path, the shine of those drivers wore off. Yes, I had an impressive resume. Yes, I had financial security and flexibility. And yes, I resented my job.

I felt like an impostor—not just the traditional impostor syndrome telling me I'm not good enough to be there but also the impostor syndrome of knowing that deep down I didn't *want* to be there. Compared to my peers, I found it difficult to feign interest. I didn't get the same energy from sitting in boardrooms (always with male leaders), sprinting through late-night financial models, or discreetly judging the nine-to-five jobs that friends held. Instead, I *daydreamed* about those nine-to-five jobs and how having one would allow me to *live* so much more of my life.

My lack of interest also affected my performance. I had a difficult time motivating myself to learn. I was scared to admit what I didn't know. And I found it difficult to compete with my peers who genuinely did love tracking markets, rubbing shoulders with executives, and wearing that badge of honor after an all-night work sprint. They were performing, while I was pretending.

Dissatisfied

I tried to make small changes. At the consulting firm, I moved from a client-facing role to an internal operating role. That improved my work-life balance, but not my engagement or satisfaction. So I made another jump. But even throughout these small adjustments, I maintained one steady thought: *This isn't it.* I started to feel desperate. *Why isn't this better? How do I fix this? Can I fix this?*

I began to allow myself to see a potential truth. Perhaps the truth was that I was in entirely the wrong arena. If that was the case, then another subtle jump—a promotion or internal move or doing the same work in a different building with a different company name—was unlikely to succeed. *I should have known*, I thought. A new mantra started to ring louder in my brain: *The definition of insanity is doing the same thing and expecting different results.*

I acknowledged the hard truth that a subtle adjustment to my job would not solve my problem. I didn't like that answer. I was comfortable with subtle career changes. I had mastered the "micro-pivot," making small changes within companies or across organizations. But an actual career pivot? To something different? A move that carries some—*gasp*—risk? That seemed daunting and scarier.

It was that fear that led me to this book. Like any good consultant, I wanted to find a repeatable framework and minimize my risk—and so my market research began. A few networking conversations led to dozens of interviews with women who made brave, bold career changes. Not just small tweaks, but big leaps! Career changes that required the confidence to say, "Yes, I will chart my own path."

GOOD THINGS HAPPEN WHEN YOU LISTEN TO YOUR GUT

The itch for more—or a feeling of disconnection with one's job—was a common theme across my interviews. Many women start a career change with the vague notion that their current job is not aligned with their authentic interests. They end up in an industry, or a role, or as part of a team, and they think, *How did I get here?* There is a desire for more, or for different. Indeed, today, two-thirds of the female workforce is wondering whether they should not just leave their jobs but change industries entirely.[1]

But what I found is that the women who were successful were those who reframed the challenge. Instead of focusing on fear and why they were unhappy in their roles (*ahem*, what I was doing in my own career journey), the most successful women instead focused on what they loved. They recommitted energy to the work that they enjoyed doing and used that as a foundation to launch their broader career transition. Take Nicole Sahin. Today Nicole is the founder and executive chair of Globalization Partners, a $1 billion company revolutionizing the way all companies hire and build global teams across the world. As a female CEO and start-up founder, she defies gender odds.

But Nicole's decision to start Globalization Partners wasn't a slam dunk, she told me. Prior to starting her company, Nicole was a leader within another player in the globalization industry. She enjoyed the work and was exhilarated by the exponential growth she helped the company achieve. The prospect of leaving her job and making a major career change to entrepreneur was nerve-racking. She was building something great, something that she loved, something that felt part of her identity. How could she ever leave?

But deep down, something was nagging at Nicole that became hard to ignore. "I want to start my own company," she heard herself saying. The benefit of Nicole's work at a fast-scaling company was that she knew she could do it. She had an entrepreneurial spirit and proved she was good at building and scaling. Knowing that, Nicole's gut was shouting at her that there was a bigger opportunity waiting for her. She could do something similar, but bigger and better.

"I just felt like I had to do it," recalled Nicole. "This mission was screaming at me and telling me it was time to move on." Many women have the intuitive feeling that Nicole describes. The difference is that not all women act on that intuition. So, what made Nicole able to take the

Dissatisfied

leap? When I asked Nicole this question, it became clear to me that she had a gift for tapping into her intuition. Throughout her career, she consistently followed the opportunities that felt authentic and truly interesting—from setting up a yoga practice in the Caribbean, to research work in Guatemala, to helping establish a school for girls in Thailand. One of Nicole's superpowers seems to be her authenticity muscle. She knows what brings her energy, which career opportunities allow her to spark magic—and she acts on them.

Nicole agrees that tapping into her authentic interests has helped her to define and pursue a career path that feels authentic and fulfilling. "What I've learned over the last many years is that whenever I follow my intuition, the better off I am. And the sooner I do it, I am able to get centered and grounded quickly." Nicole practiced what she preaches when founding Globalization Partners. As the voice inside her pushing her to start her own company surged, she made a swift and bold decision. Nicole and her husband quit their jobs. They would take one year off to travel and plant the seeds for Nicole's new venture in the globalization business.

Identifying what you really want—and then taking bold action to go after it—is not easy for all women. It was not always a strength for Nicole either. It took time for her to get comfortable listening to that voice inside her—her gut. "When I was younger, I would accept being miserable," Nicole explained. "I would just deal with it because I didn't know where I wanted to go. When you're younger, it's harder. But the more you learn about yourself as you get older, the more you know what you want and need."

Other women shared similar stories. Like Carrie Collins, who switched careers from attorney to higher education administrator. Now in the prime of her career, Carrie looks back on intuition as a key driver of her career success. "Whenever I have followed my instinct and my hunch, it has paid dividends later," Carrie told me. The benefits are twofold: following her gut accelerated Carrie's career growth *and* launched her into more fulfilling roles. Each time Carrie followed her instinct and hunch, she ended up with a unique skill set and perspective that set her apart from others. In other words, her gut led her to the things that differentiated her and made her more competitive. At the same time, her instincts also led her to work that *felt* more fulfilling.

BUT WHY IS IT SO HARD?

Many of us have stories like Nicole and Carrie where we face a fork in the road. We acknowledge we are not satisfied in our career. Then we face the decision of what to do about it. Will I take a risk and listen to my gut and heart? Or will I quiet the voice inside me and continue my path? Even for women like Nicole, who are good at listening to their intuition and honoring it with action, there is no immunity to the fear that comes with acting on your career itch. The fear is there. But women like Nicole choose to push through. "I still grapple with that fear. It's like leaping off a cliff and hoping you'll sprout wings. Now, that doesn't sound too easy. And it's not. But the idea of standing on the edge of a cliff for the rest of your life and just looking at the possibility—that feels so much worse to me."

In popular culture and among some of the most prominent businesswomen, we see this same fearlessness—women who have taken the leap. And often, that leap is driven by an initial disconnection with work. Ina Garten, the beloved Barefoot Contessa, built a food empire based on her elegant but simple cooking recipes. But before her cooking career, Ina was working in the White House. She was charging down a well-traveled path with clear trail markers and next steps—like so many women early in their careers do. But Ina found little enjoyment. "When you're in your twenties, you feel like you need to have goals and that there are so many other things you should be doing. . . . When I was in my twenties, I was working in nuclear energy policy and management and budget for the White House, thinking, 'There's got to be something more fun than this.'"[2]

Sounds familiar, right?

Ina's transition into food was based not only on intuition but, some might say, on impulse. When she saw an ad in the *New York Times* for a specialty food store for sale, she asked her husband to go look at it—but never expected she would end up purchasing it and starting her own business. Ina had never run a business, had never even had employees working for her. But when she saw the store, she realized it was the work she wanted to do. So Ina made a bold move: "I made the woman a low offer, thinking we'd have time to negotiate. But the next day she called me and said, 'I accept your offer.' That's when I said to myself, 'Oh, shoot. Now I have to run a specialty-food store.'"[3]

While we may not all have the gumption (or frankly, the option) to purchase a food store on the spot, Ina's story still has lessons for all women: Being open to career changes and listening to your gut—that voice, like Ina's, saying, "This is what I want to do"—can lead to the most fulfilling, exciting, and successful elements of your career. Staying too focused on your career track without considering the off-ramps will limit your career success. For Ina, it would have prevented her from leaving the White House, from opening her first store, and from then selling her store to start writing cookbooks. There would be no Barefoot Contessa so many know and love.

IS THIS ACTUALLY A GOOD IDEA?

We see many examples of women who have "made it" after following their gut. But these stories can feel like the diamonds in the rough. When you're a regular person forging your career, is it really a smart thing to follow your intuition and authentic interests? Is the oft-given advice to follow your passion helpful? Research suggests yes—if you do it the right way.

Despite the common tip to align career with your passion, many argue that it is not particularly helpful advice. Recent research from Stanford University shows that this advice can be detrimental for individuals, making them less successful. The problem? Following your passion implies an easy path to success. Follow your passion, and it will all snap into place! But no career trajectory is that easy or simple.

If women believe that following their passion will solve all their career challenges, they are setting themselves up to fail. Because when you do face inevitable roadblocks, you haven't expected or prepared for them, and you are more likely to give up. Focusing solely on passion also narrows your focus and makes you less likely to consider new areas of interest that may emerge over time throughout your career trajectory.[4]

So then why are we talking about aligning your career to passion or authentic interests? Because it does advance your career, if you define passion in the right way. The danger in talking about passion or authenticity alongside career is that there is a romanticized tale that one day we will wake up, embrace our passion, quit our jobs, and begin a long-term fulfilling career the next day. This is drastically oversimplified. The reality is much more nuanced.

Sometimes, following your passion is not realistic. Mark Cuban, owner of the Dallas Mavericks and star of ABC's reality television show *Shark Tank*, joked, "One of the great lies of life is 'follow your passions.' Everybody tells you, 'Follow your passion, follow your passion.' I used to be passionate to be a baseball player. Then I realized I had a seventy-mile-per-hour fastball."[5]

And even if your fastball is fast enough to make it, you may not want to make your passion your everyday work.

Research suggests that we need to change the way we see passion. Instead of a fixed, unchanging interest, such as our childhood dream of baseball, we should view passion as something to be fostered, developed, and changed throughout a career. Our career passions are plants that we water, grow, and learn to love more. In this way passion and career are intertwined and continually feed off each other. A Stanford research team suggests that passion is less something to be found, and more something to develop. As contributing researcher Paul O'Keefe describes, "If you look at something and think, 'that seems interesting,

Dissatisfied

that could be an area I could make a contribution in,' you then invest yourself in it. You take some time to do it, you encounter challenges, over time you build that commitment."[6] I like replacing the idea of "passion" with "contribution." How do you want to meaningfully contribute through your work? And how will you define contribution—based on family income, subject expertise, or social impact? Ben Horowitz, a prominent technology entrepreneur and cofounder of the venture capital firm Andreessen Horowitz, advocated for this definition change in a commencement speech: "Following your passion is a very 'me'-centered view of the world. . . . So my recommendation would be to follow your contribution. Find the thing that you're great at, put that into the world, contribute to others, help the world be better and that is the thing to follow."[7]

Replacing "follow your passion" with "go where you want to contribute" is particularly important for women, who often feel guilty or uncomfortable switching careers just for passion's sake. Career changer and author (and guest on my podcast) Jenny Blake builds on this idea in her book *Pivot*.[8] Jenny, a former Google employee who left to contribute to the spaces of career coaching and writing, encountered pangs of guilt. People would ask her, "How could you possibly leave a job at Google?" Underlying the question was the judgment that Jenny didn't have the right to evaluate her career, to want something different, to make a change—because, well, Google should be good enough.

Throughout the book you will see this type of judgment and guilt across many women's stories, like women's shame in complaining about high-paying jobs or women's guilt about leaving male-dominated industries. But these judgments are unfair and shortsighted. The reframing from passion to contribution helps assert that women's pursuit of an authentic career is not frivolous—it is purposeful, important, and value-additive to our economy and our world.

As Jenny writes in her book, that one she published after leaving Google: "Calling such career aspirations a crisis, shaming and blaming people for wanting to prioritize meaningful work in a volatile economy by saying they are 'entitled' or 'too picky,' means we are missing a huge opportunity to celebrate and support those who seek to make a greater contribution to their workplaces, society, and the lives of everyone around them."[9] Most women want to contribute to topics related to their authentic interests—the industry one woman loves, the company one woman has always wanted to start, the leadership role that allows one woman to mentor.

SO WHAT NOW?

Research shows that when people build a career based on their interests, it leads to better outcomes. Aligning interests and career leads to better career satisfaction and longer-term retention. This is true across sixty-plus studies that explore how personal interests influence job happiness, performance, and likeliness to stay in the job position. The results show a commonsense but often overlooked truth: People with jobs that align to their interests will be better performers and less likely to leave the organization.[10] If you're a business founder, your interest in and love for your business may determine success more than your skills like defining a business plan.[11] Listening to the authentic voice inside of you is a prerequisite to finding a career that is fulfilling long-term and a career in which you can thrive. For many women, hearing that voice is the first step in their career pivot. Yet it can be shockingly hard to listen up.

Women feel guilty when the voice inside their head says *I want something different; I want something more*. But no one should feel guilty for having a voice. Your authentic voice can steer you toward a career where you will make the greatest contribution, however you want to define *contribution* for yourself. If you're thinking, *I'm not like Ina or Nicole. I could never jump off a cliff or buy a grocery store without a plan*, don't worry, neither am I. Yes, some women like Nicole and Ina can easily tap into their authentic self and make swift decisions to align their career. But the reality for most women is that it's much harder.

Dissatisfied

The more common career change story is a slow burn. Women take time to open their minds to the possibility of a career change. Then over time, they diligently prepare to execute that change. Their reinvention is not an overnight sensation or an emotionally driven click of a button; it is disciplined, strategic, and incremental. In the following chapters in this section of the book, we explore how women turn up the volume on that voice and overcome guilt and fear to act. But first, another stop on the emotional journey of the career pivot: isolation, a feeling that affects so many women when considering a new career direction.

Before we examine isolation, let's take stock of where you are in your career. Are you satisfied and fulfilled in your career, or is it time to acknowledge that you are not? The following reflection exercise includes questions that help you assess where you are today and reconnect you with the parts of your career that bring energy and joy.

REFLECTION EXERCISE

1. What brings me the most energy at work?
2. How could I do more of that work?
3. How would my life change if I felt more satisfied with my career?
4. How does my feeling of dissatisfaction affect my career success?
5. What pains do I feel today? What am I dissatisfied with? What work do I dislike doing?

CHAPTER 2

ISOLATED

WHEN YOU'RE SICK OF BEING THE ONLY WOMAN

Mai Ton is an Asian American female executive who built her human resources career at big companies like PwC and exciting start-ups in hyper-growth mode. Twenty years into her career, Mai was leading HR for another growing start-up. The start-up was successful enough to move into a sleek high-rise office—the kind of "successful enough" where they had a six-figure budget *just* for their office AV equipment. When I interviewed Mai, she recalled a moment in the new office when a strange thought occurred to her as she stared out over New York City: *I thought I was happy here, but I'm not.*

This experience was so common for many women I interviewed. Women work persistently and diligently to reach the top of their career ladder, only to realize they don't like the view. But how does someone like Mai get there?

When the floor falls out from underneath them, women like Mai are both surprised and not surprised at all. On the one hand, Mai had a successful and rewarding, and sometimes thrilling, career of twenty years. On the surface, "I'm not happy" was a shock. At the same time, Mai understood her disillusionment intimately. She was simply pulling the curtain back. Mai knew that a main driver of her disillusionment was the culture that a start-up tech scene brings. The bravado of fast growth and big wins has a downside. Every start-up was homogeneous and composed of White male leaders. The start-ups subscribed to a "bro culture" that allowed for off-the-cuff jokes that ranged from insensitive to overtly racist and sexist.

Mai always recognized the lack of diversity. You know when you're the only woman or person of color in the room. But it took more to acknowledge the impact it had on her career satisfaction and fulfillment. To make the connection, Mai needed to see her work environment through fresh eyes—the eyes of her young daughter. Mai's first light bulb moment occurred when her daughter was just six years old. When a childcare shuffle between Mai and her husband fell through, Mai brought her daughter into the office for the first time. Together they attended an executive meeting, and when it ended, her daughter asked a simple question: "Mommy, why do you only work with men?"

Mai had worked in tech start-ups for decades. She was accustomed to being the only woman in the room and certainly the only woman in the leadership room. She had gotten good at sweeping this under the rug and accepting it as an inevitable condition of working in tech. However, the untarnished, optimistic eyes of her daughter changed Mai's point of view. "A six-year-old's eyes are very clear," reflected Mai. "I thought, you're right. Why *am* I the only woman in the room?" The thought burrowed into Mai's brain. She began to imagine working in an organization that was diverse, representative, and sensitive to unique viewpoints. An environment where she wouldn't hear it's just a joke—an environment where her leadership peers might look like her.

"I wanted to have a balanced executive team with diversity, or even just leaders with a high emotional quotient who didn't make insensitive jokes. I realized how much I longed for that." Mai began to test the job market. She cast a wide net, requiring only one real element—diversity in leadership and an affinity with her colleagues—to consider the opportunity. Mai knew she wanted to feel more at home, and for the first time, she would let that factor drive her search.

The problem? "I searched for it, and I never found it," recalled Mai.

Mai spent the next decade continuing her path. Now her daughter was fifteen. One day, Mai's daughter saw a picture on her phone of Mai with the team she led, out at a celebratory lunch. There were fifteen or twenty employees, a mix of men and women, who all reported to Mai. Mai's daughter looked at the picture and cocked her head. "Wait, Mom—you manage men?" Mai felt stung. Why was this a surprise to her daughter? "Yes, I do manage men!" Mai responded with pride but, more importantly, with intention. "And that can be you one day too—managing men and women and nonbinary and lots of different types of people."

WHEN ENOUGH IS ENOUGH

If Mai couldn't find the environment she yearned for, then she would build it. Thirty-five years later, with pent-up frustrations and a strong motivation to pave a new path for her daughter, Mai left her job. After thirty-five years in HR, helping others build successful career paths, today Mai is committed to finding fulfillment in hers. When I ask Mai to reflect on how her daughter inspired this new career change, there is laughter, but I also perceive sadness, perhaps regret. "Sometimes it takes an outsider perspective to make you see things more clearly. And in this case, it was my daughter," says Mai. "I didn't realize work didn't have to suck. I didn't realize I didn't have to accept working around so many men because that's just the way tech start-ups are."

Today, Mai runs a business advising HR leaders and companies and continues to operate as a chief people officer for select companies. The community she works with has dramatically changed. "I've never worked with so many women before!" Mai remarked. It is mostly women who have risen from her network, making introductions to potential clients who are also predominantly women. "I've never been exposed to so many women helping women," says Mai.

It is clear Mai has found her community. And that community has helped her to clarify her mission. This mission ties back to her daughter, who will be graduating college in a decade. A decade to go—a decade for Mai to move the dial when it comes to female leadership. "There should have been more women and more women of color at the tables with me. There should be more women at the top. I want to move things forward so my daughter doesn't have to feel the isolation and the loneliness that I felt, always being the only one at the table."

In my own career, I have experienced feelings like those Mai describes. My career is made up of tech start-ups, management consulting, and software sales. The tech start-ups and, perhaps worse, the software sales teams align with Mai's experience—male-dominated, an aggressive working culture, and borderline-to-overt sexual harassment. Even in better environments, such as management consulting firms, that in my experience genuinely strive to create equity for women, there is still lack of parity in senior positions.

Like Mai, I know what it feels like to be the only woman in the room. The only woman around for strip club jokes. The only woman in the cocktail lounge among a group of men decades older than her. When male leaders stumble over how to greet her, the one who proactively thrusts out her hand for a handshake. The only person who is required to have a trial period for a manager role when she already has people management experience. These are the most glaring examples of sexism in corporate America. But this is only the tip of the iceberg. So many more experiences are lurking underwater. As women, we are taken less seriously in corporate institutions, we have to work harder to keep up with office politics, we have to fight against being underpaid relative to our male peers, and oftentimes we will still lose out. But this type of sexism is less visible. You can't always point to it. Women feel it and know it, but institutions and men ask women: "Are you sure?"

Women then bear the additional mental burden. It becomes tiring—at some point tiring enough to give in or give up. And I entered corporate America with many privileges. I am White and straight and have no disabilities. For women entering with fewer of those privileges, existing in corporate America is even more exhausting. And the weight of operating in environments where you are "the only" adds up quicker.

BELONGING MATTERS—FULL STOP

There are many reasons that women feel disillusioned in their careers. But in almost all cases, it relates back to one fundamental theme: "My work is not aligned with my authentic self." There is a feeling among women that they don't belong. Sometimes the misalignment is between the employee and her role: "I work in a back-office function, but I get energy from engaging with customers." Or misalignment with the industry: "I work in finance, and I don't see how my work makes anyone's life better." Sometimes the misalignment is between the employee and company culture, like Mai's experience. She yearned to be her authentic self at work, but as the only woman and only woman of color in an intolerant culture, she felt like an outsider. "This is not my community. I am exhausted pretending. I am sick of feeling alone."

This third kind of misalignment, the cultural misalignment, often gets painted as a nice-to-have. Do you really need to like your office culture? Can't we just show up to our jobs, perform our tasks, and go home? But against the backdrop of today's modern workforce—where lines between work and life are blurred, where people want not only a paycheck but meaning from their job—workforce culture is critical. Each year Gallup surveys US employees on their experiences and perspectives on work, and they acknowledge the power of culture at work: "Employees expect their job to be more than a paycheck. The paycheck still matters, of course, but employees seek out and stay with organizations that have exceptional workplace cultures. And while there are numerous components of these cultures, they are often characterized by overall feelings of trust, belongingness and inclusion."[1]

Connection at work is particularly important for women. Two-thirds of women say the social aspect of a job is a major reason why they work.[2] And having genuine work connection is not a nice-to-have; it affects performance. Having strong relationships can affect how engaged women are at work. For example, women who have a best friend at work are more than twice as likely to be engaged in their job, less likely to look for other jobs, more likely to report positive daily experiences, and more likely to take risks that lead to innovation.[3]

Despite this evidence, Gallup sees that many managers believe connection and engagement are superfluous, nice-to-have elements of a work environment.[4] *Who cares about having friends at work? I care about my employees' performance*, tough-minded managers often think. But the result of Gallup's research is affirmative: Relationships affect performance. Fostering friendship can be challenging in industries and organizations with underrepresentation of all women, Black women, women of color, or LGBTQ+ women. And we see this gender and racial underrepresentation across many industries. In the United States, women make up less than 14 percent of civil engineers, 7 percent of mechanical engineers, 19 percent of software developers, 10 percent of construction managers, and 7 percent of sales workers.[5]

The tech industry often rises to the top when we discuss gender parity. Leading tech companies have committed to address pay gaps, remove bias from hiring processes, and bring in outside experts to assess internal work culture. And yet, despite all that attention to spotlight the problem, in most cases it has made little difference. As tech journalist Sarah White puts it, "Despite national conversations about gender diversity in tech, women are still underrepresented, underpaid, and often discriminated against in the tech industry."[6]

The data continues to speak for itself. Women hold only 25 percent of computing roles.[7] In Silicon Valley, women hold 11 percent of executive positions.[8] Women hold 5 percent of leadership positions in tech and comprise less than 10 percent of partners at the top one hundred venture capital firms.[9] Female candidates in hiring pools are underrepresented 16 percent of the time.[10] And women's growth trajectories in tech are stunted too, with more than 20 percent of women age thirty-five or over in junior positions.[11]

Male-dominated industries and occupations—defined as those where women make up 25 percent or less of the workforce—can make it challenging for women to thrive. These workplaces reinforce masculine stereotypes that make it difficult for women to excel.[12] Women face gendered expectations and beliefs about their leadership abilities[13] and stereotypes like "caring mother" or "office housekeeper."[14] They experience higher stress and anxiety.[15] They are more likely to lack mentorship and career development opportunities.[16] And they are exposed to higher rates of sexual harassment.[17]

WHAT DO YOU DO WHEN YOU *ARE* THE ONLY WOMAN?

How do women handle the challenges of working in a male-dominated environment, or simply in an environment where they don't belong? Women must survive, and they do develop tactics to exist in exclusive work environments. First, women distance themselves from colleagues—both male and female colleagues. Second, women accept and embrace the masculine culture around them, "acting like one of the boys" even if that is not their authentic personality. Third? Women leave.[18] Each of these strategies damages women's career trajectories. Here's how for all three.

First, withdrawing and distancing from peers prevents relationship building that we now know is so critical to engagement, success, and long-term retention. Second, adopting the prevalent male culture exacerbates and normalizes the male-dominated culture that isolates women in the first place. It also drains women, who "put on" a persona each day—a real labor and tax that women must pay to fit in. Third, when women leave the industry, they drain the already small pool of female talent. And it can harm women who don't want to leave but feel they *must*.[19]

Women face significant challenges when they are the only woman in the room. And yet there are prominent female leaders who have risen to the occasion and climbed the ranks of male-dominated organizations.

Michaela Dempsey, a VP within Fortune 1,000 company Workday—and the only woman on her executive team—has been subject to bias throughout her career. For example, early in her career a manager asked, "Why do you worry about getting promoted? You are going to get married someday." Ten years later, another manager said, "We really need to promote [male employee]. He has a new baby and is the single earner in the family."[20]

Now Michaela shares tips for women struggling to thrive in male-dominated industries. One piece of advice resonates with what I heard from women in my interviews: Be authentic. So many women struggle to bring their authentic self to work. They feel it doesn't fit in with their surroundings, which are too male, too bro, "not me." But for Michaela, it's worth the effort. Being authentic is a key part of her success, and she advises other female leaders to adopt a mindset of authenticity. While women maintain concerns about how their "female" traits may be perceived, Michaela argues that building an inauthentic presence distracts women and holds them back from success. Why?

> Because you are constantly building a work facade rather than truly focusing on the task at hand. . . . Consider how challenging it will be to progress if you're constantly putting your effort into reinventing yourself to fit the crowd around you.[21]

Authenticity matters. Like connection, it's not just a nice-to-have; it affects your career performance and advancement. When authenticity can be prioritized safely, it should be. For many women, like Mai, it takes decades to understand the importance of authenticity. It takes decades to understand the nagging truth behind "I'm not happy here." It takes decades to understand that it comes from the simple truth: "I want to be myself, but I don't belong."

EMBRACING AN UNCOMFORTABLE TRUTH

Do I feel safe enough to speak up? Can I be myself? Do I respect the people I work with? Do they respect me? When women stop to ask these kinds of questions about authenticity at work, the answers can be scary because the answer is often no. This realization frequently plants the first seeds of a career change. Tapping into the acknowledgment that the career you are living today is not allowing you to live authentically—and meet your authentic career goals—is a powerful source of self-understanding.

But it is scary. Because once you really admit to yourself the answers, it's hard to just stay where you are. And so many times these realizations—looking out over New York City and suddenly thinking, *I'm not happy here*—launch women on a new career trajectory.

Perhaps there is another story out there for me, women begin to think.

For many women, valuing authenticity can feel unnatural. For those who have focused on putting their head down and scurrying up a career ladder, pausing to reflect on satisfaction or authenticity can feel like a luxury—a luxury that they don't deserve. The next chapter explores guilt around career changes. Do you deserve to want more? Spoiler alert: The answer is yes. You'll hear the stories of women who have overcome or harnessed that guilt to move forward to a bigger and better career path.

Before we explore the emotion of guilt, spend time reflecting on your experiences as "the only" in the room. How does the work culture around you influence your career trajectory and sense of peace at work? And what does that mean for your next career step?

> **REFLECTION EXERCISE**
>
> 1. In what moments do I feel most isolated at work?
> 2. What type of people inspire me the most when it comes to my career?
> 3. How does my work environment (the people, the culture, the mission) influence my level of career success?

CHAPTER 3

GUILTY

WE'RE TOLD TO CLIMB

When I was a kid, my parents celebrated my mom's career as an attorney and encouraged me to be proud of her professional identity. In a town where many women didn't work outside the home, my parents emphasized my mom's career even more. "We need you to know that you can do anything," they seemed to implore with some desperation and panic. I was a rule follower, and I absorbed their message of empowerment. Building a career as a woman—of course, as a woman!—was paramount.

Traditional success became my goal. In school and college, this meant focusing on academics and good grades. But out in the world of jobs, what would it look like? I found myself drawn to industries and roles that seemed powerful, which also meant they seemed, well, male. I liked research, writing, and connecting with people. But, in my mind, that wouldn't get me far on my quest to become a high-powered career woman.

I wondered what the "business" thing was all about. I had taken just one business class in college, and as I mentioned, it was the only course

I dropped. And yet business seemed to be the epitome of power. And so I started my career in a technology start-up working on traditional business projects across strategy, partnerships, and business development. It was a male environment, particularly across leadership, with an aggressive culture that favored a zero-sum competitive mentality and where I heard more than one joke about women and strip clubs (to paint a picture).

But I wanted to keep climbing the business ladder. I felt that as a woman, particularly a woman who was "faking it until making it" without a traditional business background, more credentials would help. I thought a degree from an elite business school would prove that I deserved to stay in the club. So I applied to MBA programs. During my MBA program at MIT, I kept thinking, *How can I climb more rungs? How can I be one of "them" up there at the top?* And so I stepped onto the next traditional rung of the ladder that was overpopulated by White men: management consulting. I earned a job at one of the top three firms beloved by MBA students and recruiters hiring talent.

I had arrived. Tech start-ups, business school, elite management consulting—I had earned my spot in communities and clubs where men operate with more power. *And I felt empty.*

WE'RE TOLD TO BE GOOD FEMINISTS

When women consider a career pivot, it is natural to worry that a change will slow your ascent up the corporate ladder—or whatever ladder you're climbing. *Will I have to take a step back? Will it take me more time to get back to where I am today?* This reflection is logical, and it can be valuable—you *do* need to strategize about your path. However, it is also where more damaging thoughts surface and negatively influence women's perspectives on their career trajectory.

One of the most common thoughts that women have earlier in a career transition is guilt. There is a particular breed of guilt—feminist guilt—that comes into play. Feminist guilt is the form of guilt women feel when they worry how their personal career decision will affect the

Guilty

broader advancement of women as a gender. *What will this mean for other women at my company? How will my choice affect my daughter and her generation?*

Women are influenced by the cultural messages they hear growing up. And for many women hitting their career stride today, they are part of the generation that absorbed the cultural message that they should persist and work hard—often harder than their male counterparts—to establish a career outside of the home. These women are in the senior stages of their career and feel they are the first generation with true access to corporate careers. Or they are millennial women who watched their mothers fight to have it all and are now grappling with how to have it all in their own life and career.

These "lean in" career messages have been empowering for many women. But they also create pressure and expectations that are distracting—distracting from what is the right individual decision for each woman. Women feel deep pressure to prove that they, and their generation, are contributing to the feminist cause and progression of women. It is not surprising that women feel this burden, because some form of the message is everywhere.

Sheryl Sandberg catapulted this brand of self-empowerment feminism into women's hearts and minds with her 2013 book *Lean In: Women, Work, and the Will to Lead*.[1] While Sandberg acknowledged the challenges of balancing work and life as a woman, her general philosophy was to keep going. Literally, to lean in. She urged women to keep their foot on the gas pedal and stake out a seat at the table. Her general point of view? Make it work.

Sheryl's point of view put more pressure and more guilt on women to lean in, at any cost. But why? Why do Sheryl Sandberg and other women cling to the self-empowerment point of view? The answer is rooted in feminist guilt. As *Atlantic* journalist Debora Spar writes, "Why is this happening? Because women born in the wake of feminism—women like [Sheryl] Sandberg, [Anne-Marie] Slaughter, and me—have been subtly striving all our lives to prove that we have picked up the torch that feminism provided. That we haven't failed the mothers and grandmothers who made our ambitions possible."[2]

Anne-Marie Slaughter is another name I think of alongside Sheryl Sandberg. Anne-Marie—Princeton and Harvard law graduate, law professor, State Department policy planning director, head of a major think tank, tapped by Hillary Clinton to serve in one of the most important State Department roles—had climbed high on the professional and political ladder. Anne-Marie embodied the lean-in philosophy to a tee.

Yet many people learned of Anne-Marie only when she published a viral article in 2012 shortly before *Lean In* was published. The article was titled "Why Women Still Can't Have It All." It went viral, earning over three million views because it struck a controversial chord among elite, high-powered women ambitiously forging ahead in their careers. The women to whom Sheryl Sandberg was about to preach her *Lean In* sermon. The women who had been told they could have it all. What now?[3]

The title of Anne-Marie's article, "Why Women Still Can't Have It All," sums up the main point: Even ambitious, high-charging, and privileged women have the odds stacked against them when it comes to having it all. The few women who are able to balance motherhood and being top professionals are either superhuman, rich, or self-employed.[4] Anne-Marie's ideology changed because she learned the lesson herself. In 2011, she left a high-profile foreign policy job in the State Department and returned to her hometown to be closer to her family and two teenage sons. Once the woman who embodied having it all, Anne-Marie had reached a different conclusion: The juggling act was impossible. Her maniacal work ethic focused on having it all—driven by feminist guilt to prove she could make it work—was an unrealistic standard, not only for herself but also as a standard for the many women and girls who looked up to her.

As she writes in the article, the penny dropped. Anne-Marie's belief that women could have it all—a belief she preached to other women coming up in the ranks—was upended. She realized that this was not a realistic or productive message to be sending to the women looking up to her generation or listening to her lectures. And she understood the damage this message had done. "I'd been part, albeit unwittingly, of making millions of women feel that they are to blame if they cannot manage to rise up the ladder as fast as men and also have a family and an active home life (and be thin and beautiful to boot)."[5]

Anne-Marie's network of high-powered women urged her not to publish the article. They were clinging to this feminist narrative, and they didn't want to let go. Anne-Marie describes one friend's reaction to the article as horrified. The friend worried that a statement coming from Anne-Marie—a role model for career-oriented women—would be a harmful signal to younger women coming up in the ranks of their careers.

It took two more years for Anne-Marie to muster the courage, break from her longstanding feminist narrative, and share her new truth. She knew it was time to talk, for real. The women of Anne-Marie's generation had clung to a feminist credo centered on moving up the ranks at any cost. But Anne-Marie's peers were falling out of the ranks in greater and greater numbers, as impossible trade-offs between family and career forced them to let go. Not only was this credo unrealistic; the next generation knew it was unrealistic, too, and they had stopped listening.[6]

INSTEAD, CHOOSE YOURSELF

Striving to be a part of the feminist progression—to not let our mothers and previous generations down—rings true in so many of the stories of women I interviewed. Take Melynda Barnes. Melynda's initial career is one that Sheryl Sandberg and early Anne-Marie Slaughter would praise. Melynda has a medical degree with clinical experience at many of the best hospital systems in the world. She became a talented facial plastic surgeon, one of the most coveted specialties in the medical world and a specialty in which women are severely underrepresented. Melynda, indeed, had climbed the ladder and broken some glass ceilings along the way.

But Melynda felt something was missing from her clinical career. Melynda loves innovation. She loves entrepreneurship. She loves tackling problems and finding different ways to do things better. A clinical role did not provide much space for those opportunities. She had an itch to think bigger and kept returning to the idea of being not only a doctor but somehow a connector between the medical world and the business world that addressed innovation and tackling new problems. And so, in the middle of her career, Melynda resigned. With no next step figured out, she submitted her resignation letter and said goodbye to her clinical practice.

"It was really, really hard and scary to submit that resignation letter. I didn't have a job lined up, and people thought I was crazy. 'Why are you doing this?' they would ask me in shock." Melynda feared that her choice would affect her reputation and the way her colleagues would perceive her. Would they think she was a failure or assume she was leaving because she wasn't a good doctor?

But even more than her individual reputation, Melynda suffered from feminist guilt. Melynda had reached a high rung on the ladder. And not only had she done it, but she had also shown that you can do it as a woman. As a surgeon, she was breaking ground in a field where women are severely underrepresented, less than 15 percent of the workforce.[7] "I felt guilty for walking away from a career that so many people were fighting so hard to have. I thought, *Am I being selfish?*"

Melynda's identity as a Black woman only increased her concerns. While women are underrepresented in plastic surgery, women of color are *drastically* underrepresented.[8] Few women of color go into medicine, fewer into surgery, and even fewer into plastic surgery. The result? Melynda saw herself as a role model and felt an obligation to pay it forward. Not only did *she* feel this pressure, but others added to the pressure. She imagined her peers and executives asking, "How could you leave? Everywhere you walk in this hospital, you're a role model." This guilt about potentially letting students and doctors down was the most painful part of Melynda's decision.

Melynda's conviction that she had another calling was too strong to ignore. She knew her current role was not her career purpose. She was doing great work and helping provide quality care to people, but she wanted to help people at true scale and knew she would need to get into technology and innovation to achieve that. The day after her resignation, she felt relief. "I woke up and felt like I could take a deep breath, and the hope, anticipation, and excitement started right away. There was horrible pain in considering moving on, but once the words were spoken and I had said my piece, I felt relief. I felt free to explore what freedom looks like for me, and I realized no one has to wake up and be me every day but me."

Melynda moved on to join Ro, a healthcare start-up company disrupting medical care through telemedicine. Today she is the chief medical officer. She is energized by Ro's mission to deliver healthcare in a fresh, new way that fixes an often-broken healthcare system. She does not doubt her decision to ignore the guilt and follow her gut. "It's been amazing. Not to sound too metaphysical, but I feel like my soul and purpose are in alignment. I'm actually doing what I am supposed to do."

As for her guilt around supporting other physicians, particularly women and people of color? Melynda has learned that she doesn't need to sacrifice. She remains an active mentor to women and doctors of color. In her new role, she believes she has more time and more visibility. This allows her to help *more* people on their pathways within the medical world. Not only can she teach them about dermatology and facial plastics, but now she can teach on healthcare delivery and how physicians can be empowered in their careers.

LOOK BEYOND THE LADDER

Helping women advance in their careers is a powerful motivator for women. Almost all the women I interviewed love coaching and mentoring women, especially the next generation. Projecting a message that women *can* get to the top of the ladder is important. It tells young girls that anything is possible. It motivates women to invest early in their career. It can sustain middle-age or later-stage women to keep on going. It is important.

But it can also be harmful because it restrains and inhibits women from finding the best career path *for them*. The self-empowerment narrative prescribes a definition of success that is limited. Yes, proving that women can get to the top of the ladder is an element of success, but it's not the only one. For women who define success differently, feminist guilt pushes them into a box that may never set them up for the broader success they envision: aligning career with authentic interests, balancing career with personal passions, building a family, and defining what motherhood looks like as a few examples.

And even for women who *want* to get to the top of the ladder, feminist guilt is limiting. If women don't feel that they are allowed to step off their traditional career ladder, then their options for growth are limited. Instead, they are confined to the limits of whatever ladder they were told to start climbing. Don't miss the irony: Sometimes a relentless commitment to reach the top of the ladder *prevents* women from reaching their highest success. Taking a step off the ladder—sideways, back a couple of steps, or to the ladder a few rows over—often has the potential to launch women further and faster in their career.

Like Melynda: Her first step off the plastic surgery ladder was terrifying. Everyone told her, "Don't quit." Somehow, in spite of everyone around her, Melynda found the courage to step off the ladder. Today, she has moved into a greater leadership role with arguably more opportunity to accumulate wealth, influence, and professional success. And, still a feminist, in her new position she can reach down and grab *more* women and women of color to pull them up. Finally, and not to be deprioritized, Melynda is in a career where she feels purposeful, invested, and aligned. Without the bravery to go against the advice of those around her, Melynda would be hanging steady (and probably burned out and disillusioned) on her previous ladder. The plastic surgeon ladder is not a bad one. But the ladder Melynda is climbing today is a better one *for her.*

Feminist guilt is not the only guilt that women experience when considering a career change. The next chapter talks about socioeconomic guilt. Socioeconomic guilt also holds women back from believing they have the right to forge whatever career path is best for them. Just like feminist guilt, socioeconomic guilt limits women's career paths and ultimately holds them back from their greatest career potential.

If you grapple with guilt when it comes to your career, spend time responding to the questions below. You are in charge of your career, and like Melynda, only you will wake up every day to do your work. Start understanding the guilt you might be holding on to and whether it truly is serving you.

REFLECTION EXERCISE

1. Who has a right to be a decision maker when it comes to my career?
2. How will a career change allow me to contribute or create impact in my community?
3. What truths would become clear if I were to focus only on myself?

CHAPTER 4

RELUCTANT

WE'RE TOLD WE HAVE IT "GOOD ENOUGH"

Many women I interview hesitate to pivot their career because they feel it is an act of privilege. They feel guilty that their current path doesn't feel like enough. They feel ashamed that they perceive there's something more out there waiting for them. The guilt is tied to a sense of financial or socioeconomic values. It often hits hardest for women from working- or middle-class backgrounds. When a woman has a stable and well-paying job, it feels selfish to question or complain about that career foundation. Women self-criticize their desire for more or their curiosity to explore. *What right do I have to complain about a steady, consistent job?* they think. Yet they continue to feel disengaged, unmotivated, and unfulfilled.

Socioeconomic guilt impedes women from demanding more in their career. Often the guilt is strong enough to shut down a career change before it even starts. Guilt suppresses the other feelings that women have—their doubts, dissatisfaction, frustrations. *I should be happy enough in the job that I have. I've got benefits. I've got decent pay. I'm able to put food on the table. That's enough.*

But is it enough?

Financial compensation is an important part of any job, especially for women who want to have financial independence and freedom. Financial considerations are inevitable, and they can be a positive motivator for many women. Financial reward drives women toward careers that provide financial stability and independence, for example. However, financial pressure can also be a negative force that keeps women from pursuing a career that is authentic and fulfilling. Women may prioritize the benefits of a well-paying job over their level of interest or engagement with the work. Pay is often rewarding in the short term but can limit your career trajectory long term. Aligning your authentic interests with your career often drives greater career success. And it can set up women for longer-term financial success by putting them in a role where they can thrive, maximizing their income over the long term.

WHAT SOCIOECONOMIC GUILT LOOKS LIKE

Michelle Obama recounts her experience with socioeconomic guilt in her memoir, *Becoming*, where she narrates the personal and career pivots she made throughout her life. Michelle acknowledges the major influence that her socioeconomic background had on her decisions. She grew up on the South Side of Chicago with working-class parents in a tough community that didn't always expect much of her. But Michelle had supportive parents and was intrinsically motivated to make something of herself. A "box checker" who put her head down and followed the rules, she worked hard in school and went on to graduate from Princeton University and Harvard Law School and land a coveted attorney position at a law firm paying rich six-figure salaries and extra bonuses.[1]

Armed with Princeton and Harvard degrees, sitting in a fancy corporate high-rise, and working for a prestigious law firm—by all accounts, Michelle had made it. She had checked every box and reached the top of the ladder. She had fulfilled the dreams she worked so hard for since her childhood in Chicago. The end results? "I hated being a lawyer. I wasn't suited to the work. I felt empty doing it, even if I was plenty good at it."[2] Like so many women who make it to the top, Michelle felt dissatisfied. The work lacked purpose. Her achievement felt empty. She had the coveted view from the top of the ladder, but did it even mean anything?

But complicating these feelings was Michelle's sense of socioeconomic guilt. How could she complain about a job that so many of her peers would never come close to? It felt indulgent to question the opportunity in front of her and the position she was fortunate to have.

She stayed in the job for some time but still felt disillusioned. Michelle went to her mother for perspective. She shared her feelings about her work, telling her mother she was not happy in the job. She didn't feel it was her passion. The work felt empty. Expecting a sympathetic ear, Michelle instead was hit with a different reality that reflects the deep socioeconomic pressure and guilt embedded in so many women growing up middle class, poor, or financially stressed.

Michelle's mother's advice? "Make the money, worry about being happy later." And with these words, Michelle's socioeconomic guilt hit her like a ton of bricks. "I was like [gulps], Oh. Okay. Because how indulgent that must have felt to my mother. . . . When she said that, I thought, *Wow—what—where did I come from, with all my luxury and wanting my passion?* The luxury to even be able to decide—when she didn't get to go back to work and start finding herself until after she got us into high school."[3] Michelle's guilt contributed to her career inertia. Her dissatisfaction with her job, indeed, seemed like a luxury. Could she really question a job so prestigious, so well-paid, one that her parents could have only dreamed of? Plus, Michelle's contemplation came at a time when her success and stability was uncertain. President Obama was not a political rock star, not yet recognized as a future presidential candidate. Michelle had no crystal ball to predict the future opportunities she would have, either—First Lady, a best-selling book, paid speaking engagements, and her choice of work as a sought-after and beloved global phenomenon.

LEAP

If Michelle couldn't allow herself to question her job as an attorney because of her socioeconomic guilt, how could she possibly act to change it?

THE POWER OF FINANCIAL SECURITY

While Michelle's story is exceptional in its achievements—not all of us are Harvard Law graduates and certainly not the First Lady—the socioeconomic guilt Michelle feels is common to many of us. I think of my own mom. She grew up in a blue-collar household; her dad was a butcher and the owner of a small grocery store, and her mom raised the kids and occasionally worked retail jobs at stores like Hallmark. When my mom looked at the world around her childhood, she saw limitations. She set her sights on achieving more. She became a first-generation college graduate, earned her law degree, and settled into a corporate legal job where she earned a salary higher than what she ever imagined possible growing up.

When I interviewed my mom about her legal career, she said that she was initially satisfied; in fact, she was thrilled and highly motivated. She was grateful for a white-collar job with competitive pay and benefits. That translated to a commitment to her work and the desire to go above and beyond. She was thrilled to have this kind of job and motivated to keep it. "I was incredibly excited about the job. It was a very legitimate role. It was in a big organization; I felt like I was in a world that I had not been a part of before. I felt like I had a lot to live up to, so I was super motivated."

But day by day, the shininess of my mom's legal career dulled, until years later, she woke up and finally acknowledged that she was no longer happy in her job. She was working long hours but felt like she achieved little impact or true change in the organization. It seemed that everyone showed up just to play a part. She looked around at her peers and saw that she was working harder than everyone else. But it all felt meaningless. She had fought for entry into this new corporate world with all its privileges and benefits, but now that she was there, it didn't mean she *liked* it.

When I talked to my mom, she described how her socioeconomic concerns kept her rooted in the job for years to come. Her parents (my grandparents) had instilled in her a strong work ethic. And their jobs and lives, which felt modest to my mom as a child, motivated her to push toward new heights. "I grew up with messages around me about getting ahead. The message was that you push, you pull—you do whatever you can to climb upward." My mom didn't feel she had the right or the luxury to consider a change. She was simply focused on climbing the ladder toward a higher rung, at work and in her life.

My mom's socioeconomic guilt was not unfounded; it was rooted in financial realities. My mom's salary offered her stability, freedom, and experiences that she never had growing up. Making a career change filled my mom with fear that she would give up that financial security. That security and freedom were *worth it*. But at some point, my mom's fear of losing that security was no longer rooted in reality. My mom's income over the years, alongside my dad's income, provided our family with enough savings to have long-term financial security—regardless of the career choices my mom made or didn't make. But socioeconomic guilt and fear is hard to let go of, and my mom clung to it: "I always feared that my sense of financial security would be short-lived, and if I gave up the legal job, I would regret it. If you've had a time in your life when you've gone to bed at night and put your head on the pillow and not felt financially secure—especially when you're a child—it really imprints on you. That fear is real. It makes you feel nervous."

WHAT IT TAKES TO LEAP

While the seeds of dissatisfaction were planted early on, my mom didn't leave her legal career until later. When both of her aging parents became sick within a short period of time, she took a sabbatical. That sabbatical turned into a resignation. She spent two years frequently on the road, driving to support her aging parents while continuing to raise my siblings and me. At the same time, on a whim, my mom started volunteering with students at a high school. She saw the volunteer posting while reading the newspaper during one of her hospital visits with my sick grandfather. My mom remembers that something called out to her—she was drawn to the idea of helping others at a time when she felt helpless in her own life. She called the number on the posting and began her volunteer role.

When both of my grandparents passed away in short succession, my mom planned to return to her legal career. She asked around her network for job opportunities and arranged her first interview. It turned out to be the interview that would change the course of her career.

The interview was for an attorney position at a small law firm. My mom remembers that the hiring attorney she met with was kind and competent and the job offered a competitive salary and flexibility. This job had all the key ingredients. And yet, as my mom walked out of the interview, one thing was clear: she absolutely did not want the job. "There was nothing about a legal job that was impressive to me anymore. It didn't have the meaning of 'making it' and 'achieving' that I was so eager for earlier in my career. The shine was off. I remember coming home and admitting to your dad, 'God, I hope this guy doesn't give me the offer.'"

My dad shared my mom's experience of growing up in a middle-class household that instilled a value of financial hustle and achieving more than what you grew up with. He shared the same sense of socioeconomic pressure as my mom. So he had the same instincts to take the job and make the money. But in this instance, he gave my mom surprising advice. "If you don't want the job, you should hurry up and let him know. Because if he calls you back and officially offers you a job, you know you're going to take it," he said.

Reluctant

Both my parents knew that the socioeconomic guilt and fear—those currents that had influenced my mom's entire career to date—would compel her to take the job. Both had the same mentality that if you get offered an opportunity to make money, you don't turn it down. If she got the offer, they wouldn't say no. My mom took my dad's advice and never let the job offer come her way. She contacted the firm to let them know she did not want to proceed. After that, my mom went on a few more law firm interviews, but each time she came home discouraged. She felt sunken, devoid of joy, and thought, *This is just not what I want to do.*

My mom remembers that she couldn't help but compare her feelings leaving law firm interviews to what she felt when she was volunteering. She was volunteering during a challenging time in her life as she watched both of her parents deteriorate and eventually pass away, and yet her volunteer work had been a joyful time. Working with students provided a sense of purpose and impact. The experiences of being an attorney and working with students were totally different. Every time my mom walked in to teach and work with students, she got a warm feeling. She knew the legal jobs she was interviewing for would never give her that same experience.

Throughout my mom's career, the strongest guiding influence was her socioeconomic guilt and financial insecurity. *You are the daughter of a small shop owner. Who are you to complain about your job as an attorney? To want something different? To imagine something more?* But decades later, on the heels of the loss of her parents, my mom finally considered listening to a different voice inside of her head. And this voice was telling her to follow her gut, to acknowledge the joy she was experiencing in her volunteer work, and to let that lead.

So she made a change, ending her legal career and starting fresh in her fifties. She returned to graduate school to earn a teaching degree and spent the following twelve years teaching high school students. I remember coming home from college to attend her graduation from grad school. As a college student, I was absorbed in my own life. But even then, I felt the significance of this moment. *My mom isn't afraid of taking a different path* was a feeling that continues to stick with me. And though my mom did pivot to a more authentic and joyful career, it took an extraordinary number of circumstances to move her beyond her guilt. She waited until she had bullet-proofed her financial security. Even then, she needed something more—the gravity of the death of her parents—to finally give herself permission to let go of the message to always keep climbing up. For the first time, she embraced the possibility that there might be other, stronger messages to follow when it comes to her career and her life.

For other women, is there a way to get there sooner?

ALIGN YOUR CAREER TO YOUR VALUES

Like my mom, many women hesitate to question their career path because it feels like a privileged act. For women who climb up the ladder to a spot that is higher than their childhood expectations or what their parents or peers achieved, it can feel ungrateful to question their position. And along with the guilt, there is a new emotion: fear. It is terrifying to give up that position especially when you are one of the first to have reached it. I've been there. I have worked at some of the best businesses and companies in the world. *What more could I possibly be looking for? And what will happen if I give up this spot on the ladder? If I do something different, will I ever reach this height again?*

Socioeconomic fear is part of my story too. I wanted to earn a lot of money because I value financial freedom—the apple doesn't fall far from the tree when it comes to my mom, I suppose. I saw the financial fear my parents had grown up with, and I wanted to avoid it at all costs. And as a feminist, I thought it was important that I earn the same (or more) than my male peers. But compensation became my ultimate—sometimes my only—measure of being at the top. I benchmarked what was enough money not by what I needed, but by what I had relative to others. I never consciously thought about my relationship with money and what I wanted it to be; instead, I took on my parents' financial narrative and relationship with money as my own reality too. But when you have this dynamic with money, no amount will ever be enough. Chasing a number that always grows is exhausting. And at some point, I realized I didn't want money to be the only factor in my career decisions. I wanted to feel meaning in my work. I wanted to contribute through my work. I wanted to be sharing my talents through my work. At some point, I wanted more from my career than just a paycheck. But when that truth bubbled up, I reverted to guilt, as many women do. *Why can't making money be enough of a motivator for me? Am I lazy? Am I entitled? A bad person?*

When these feelings hit, we want to stuff the genie back into the bottle. We feel shameful for even letting them out. This was perfectly articulated for me in the book *Pivot* by Jenny Blake. Jenny left Google to start her own company and write a book. The hardest part was the judgment she felt from the world around her. "You're leaving GOOGLE?" She questioned her decision and her legitimate right to make a change. As Jenny describes, "We start to internalize some of this shame and blame that we feel from the outside world. 'You're so lucky; I would kill for this job!'—I used to get this a lot. All of a sudden it seems unreasonable to talk about what's really going on and how you might really be feeling."[4]

But new research and thought leadership are exploring people's decisions to leave well-paying and prestigious jobs. And among the career types that are high up on the ladder—attorneys, bankers, or big tech workers—a consistent theme emerges: "Graduates who flock to Wall Street, Silicon Valley, and big law in search of prestige might be in for a harsh wake-up call only a few years later."[5] People on these tracks are more frequently reaching the middle or late stage of their careers to find that the prestige is not fulfilling. Once reluctant to consider anything outside a traditional prestigious track, these individuals end up feeling deeply lost and disillusioned.

Indeed, more experienced employees in their mid or late careers tend to prioritize factors *not* related to prestige. For example, when making a career change at an older age, individuals are more likely to move into less prestigious occupations.[6] As a *Forbes* contributing career coach described, many clients reach a point where they tire of climbing the ladder *just to climb the ladder*. They have "checked all the boxes of what it was supposed to be like to have a really good career, and they didn't feel like they wanted to continue down that path just for the sake of continuing down that path."[7]

So why do people flock to the prestige path in the first place? Why are we so reluctant to build a career centered on our authentic skills and interests? Well, there are real benefits to prestigious careers: high pay, job security, opening doors down the road, and in the best cases, important and challenging work. But there are also more insidious factors that drive women to choose prestige. One of the most common is a desire for the external approval that you get from others. In fact, *prestige* is defined as the "distinction or reputation attaching to a person or thing and thus possessing a cachet for others or for the public."[8]

Though it's alluring to seek external approval, the pursuit of only prestige and socioeconomic status can guide women on a path that ends up unfulfilling—because they pursued a path that *they* never really wanted. Harvard psychologist Susan David studies this topic and how it leads people to live *someone else's* dreams instead of their own. "We can often land up being in a way in our lives where we turn around and we say, 'How did I get here?' I was just going on with the flow. I was just doing what everyone else told me to do."[9] We end up achieving success, but we don't feel happy or fulfilled in the way we had hoped. And yet it's still hard to leave. Even when we know we are on the wrong path, we are reluctant to veer from it. And we may stay on it for a long time.

HOW TO AVOID GETTING ON THE WRONG PATH

So how can women avoid getting on the wrong path? Can we find a way to pivot onto the right trajectory earlier so we can avoid years of unfulfillment and stagnation when we are too reluctant to make a change? The challenge is usually *not* that women know what will fulfill them but actively ignore it. Instead, often women truly don't know what matters to them when it comes to work because they never make space or time to consider it. They never pause to reflect on what type of career will feel worthwhile and will be sustained over a long period of time. They are reluctant to even *consider* a different possibility.

Susan David studies how simple reflection exercises or "values-affirmation" exercises that ask basic questions about work and value—What did I do today that was worthwhile? If today was my last day on earth, what would I have done that was worthwhile?—can affect career success and performance.[10] And there is research to show that there is a connection between the two. For example, one study shows that people perform better in challenging situations when they complete the values exercise prior to the activity.[11] A similar study shows that first-generation college students who complete the values exercise earn better grades than peers.[12] There are similar results for female surgical residents who, after completing the values exercise, perform better on clinical evaluations.[13]

This type of values exercise, which typically involves naming and writing about the things that are important to you, helps quiet the biases and traditional wisdom around you. Instead, you can start from your personal experience to define your career path. This path is better aligned to you as an *individual*. The exercise helps you translate abstract values into concrete actions. When you articulate what is most important to you, you are more likely to make decisions with those factors in mind. As Susan writes, you are "more likely to cultivate habits that are congruent with who you want to be in the world."[14] When you have a clearer sense of what you want in your career, you are less reluctant—and more likely—to go after your goals.

While both women and men can struggle to identify core values for their career, women face particular challenges. Women are often not fully encouraged to explore and achieve their full ambition. Instead, beginning in early childhood, our world tells women and girls to limit their goals to stay within traditional gender roles and expectations. Author Chimamanda Ngozi Adichie describes this sentiment in her popular TEDx Talk and essay "We Should All Be Feminists": "We teach girls to shrink themselves, to make themselves smaller. We say to girls, you can have ambition, but *not too much*. You should aim to be successful, but not *too* successful."[15] We tell women that what they have is good enough. We tell women to be reluctant.

Even when women ignore these messages and continue to work for a fully expressed career, their ambition and efforts are often suppressed at pivotal points in their career. When women are overlooked for promotions, when they earn less than their male counterparts, when they carry an uneven burden of childcare and family labor—their ambition is battered. They start to wonder, *How much do I really want this?* But this is not because women inherently lack ambition—a deeply misplaced perspective used to position this as something women, rather than systemic institutions, need to fix. Women do have career ambition, just as much as their male counterparts. But they might lose that ambition when they find themselves climbing the ladder within systems and organizations that work against them. In other words, an ambition gap between men and women exists *only* in the organizations "where women see an uphill battle to reach an unattractive summit."[16]

REVAMPING GUILT AND FEAR

Socioeconomic guilt and feminist guilt are closely tied to fear. As women, we fear the judgment of others. We fear letting our communities down. We fear failing. We fear we will make a mistake. We fear that we can't turn back. All of this fear makes us reluctant. It feels easier, simpler, and safer to just stay put. But women must shed guilt and fear when it comes to planning for and executing a long-term career. Women have *the right* to pursue a meaningful career. Desiring a fulfilling career does not mean that women are ungrateful. They are not acting out of selfishness or privilege. Career changes are a strategic and inevitable part of evolving in today's fluid career economy, even sometimes when they require a step down. Pivots are also a strategic part of ensuring that women engage in meaningful work that aligns with not just their jobs, but how they want to live their lives.

Fear makes women think small. We are reluctant to pivot our careers because we focus on what we might leave behind. But what if we focus on what we might gain? That's thinking big. When women think big, that's where the magic happens. In the next chapter, we explore women's relationship with fear, why fear is the most common emotion for women reinventing their careers, and how many rockstar women have learned to harness fear to their benefit.

I want all women to better understand how fear and financial concerns affect their career decisions. Money and the value you get from your work is an important part of all career decisions. But as women, we need to make sure that our financial goals do not create such reluctance to take a risk that we accept the status quo as the best we'll ever have—and never challenge ourselves to move ahead to bigger and better career opportunities.

REFLECTION EXERCISE

1. How will you know when you have achieved financial security? Will it make you less hesitant when it comes to your career?

2. When you are reluctant to consider a change, what opportunities are you saying no to?

3. If you could devote your career to anything and still have the money and lifestyle you needed, what would you be doing with your career?

CHAPTER 5

AFRAID

THE UNAVOIDABLE EMOTION

Nearly all women face the same emotions when they contemplate a career change. Women often sense there is something more they want out of their careers, but they struggle to understand their authentic career interests—and so they are left feeling uncertain about how or where to start. The longer they stay in their existing careers, the lonelier and more frustrated they feel, especially those in male-dominated work cultures. Women feel shameful for considering leaving behind a corporate position that previous generations of women fought so hard to have access to. Or they are reluctant to leave behind a traditional, securely compensated path. In addition to all these emotions, there is one feeling that *all* women I interviewed shared in common. Literally, every single woman. That feeling?

Fear.

Making a major career pivot is a terrifying prospect. And it's terrifying for so many reasons. There is the risk of leaving behind an established path or job with clear markers to follow. There is the worry of judgment or disapproval from peers and other people. There is the uncertainty of success when taking on something new. There is the fear of betting on themselves. Every single woman I researched or interviewed has a story to tell about fear.

Fear is different than reluctance. Reluctance is what keeps us from considering a change in the first place. But fear is what kicks in when we know we want something, but we struggle to take that first step.

We've seen fear in the stories of women shared in earlier chapters. Melynda Barnes, the plastic surgeon, worried deeply about how leaving behind her medical career would influence other women, particularly women of color, trying to make it. My mom held on to a dissatisfying career because she was afraid to let go of a stable salary. Even when she had enough financial security to allow for a lower-paying job, she couldn't let go of the reluctance that comes from growing up financially insecure.

In every woman's story that comes later in the book, you will also hear an account of fear. But luckily many women also told me how they were able to positively harness fear instead of just letting fear hold them back.

FINANCIAL FEAR AND TAKING RISKS

When it comes to women and career changing, there are different shades of fear. One of the most common types of fear is financial fear. Financial fear is different than socioeconomic guilt or financially driven reluctance, which we talked about in previous chapters. Even when we overcome the guilt and reluctance around wanting *more* than just a paycheck from your job, we still need to tackle the *fear* that comes with actually taking that step forward and risking financial security.

Leaving the stability of a corporate paycheck is one of the biggest risks women face when considering a career pivot. This is especially true for entrepreneurs and solopreneurs who must rely on themselves to generate revenue. Claire Krawsczyn was considering a pivot from a corporate public relations career to launching her own communications firm. But as a self-proclaimed non–risk taker, leaving a steady corporate job was frightening—almost paralyzing. This was particularly true since Claire was an equal earner alongside her husband and would eventually become the single household income.

Claire had seen the women in her life (peers, friends, family) stick to the comforts of a traditional career path. But she also saw that these women were so unhappy because their decision was based on a willingness to deprioritize their individual interests and career ambition. "Women are not used to putting things at risk for their own personal benefit. To give up benefits like health insurance and a stable income and long-term savings to take a risk and step outside—we've really been taught that would go against the grain," she told me. For Claire, the stability of climbing a traditional career ladder was tempting. She couldn't imagine putting at risk so much stability and security. "The risky part was giving up all of the security that came with a really, really straightforward career path," she explained.

Some research suggests that women behave more conservatively than men when it comes to finances. Women are less willing to take investment risks and more likely to be afraid of financial insecurity, job insecurity, and overspending. This is not all bad—women tend to be pragmatic with their money. When given extra hypothetical money, women prioritize valuable things like savings, reducing debt, and spending on their children. Put in other words, "[Women] are less willing to take risks with money than men, but they'll ensure the mortgage is paid off."[1] However, a less obvious consequence of women's pragmatism is the impact on long-term financial success. Women tend to prioritize tangible day-to-day expenses over long-term investments, for example.

The focus on the day-to-day and needs right in front of your face applies to career too. Women like Claire are so focused on their daily job responsibilities—and for mothers, pair that with a tremendous number of care-related responsibilities—that it's common to only look one or two steps ahead, if that. But the absence of a long-term plan—three, four, even five steps ahead—can limit women's career trajectories. Just like women need to look beyond daily savings to plan for long-term savings and retirement when it comes to their finances, women also should plan for their long-term career goals.

The good news is that while many studies depict men as bigger risk takers,[2] a newer wave of research suggests it's not that simple. Risk-taking cannot be trivialized merely to gender norms. Gender differences in risk-taking often exist, but they are a product of socialization—the way that we raise girls versus boys, rather than a biological difference. A woman's appetite for risk-taking (in this case, a girl's appetite) depends on the dominant culture around them. Girls change their risk-taking based on the preferences and cultural norms in which they exist.[3]

Another way to look at it? Our appetite for risk is malleable.[4] If we change the narrative around what we expect from women when it comes to risk, then women's behavior will change too.

AFRAID OF BEING AN IMPOSTOR

Most women who are considering a career change face another powerful fear: *Do I have the right skill set to pivot?* Inherent in every pivot is a level of change in job responsibilities and the skills required. If you're not changing any of the responsibilities or skills, then it's not a pivot. So it's inevitable that women face a skills gap between their "before" and "after" jobs. For many women, this is a vulnerable time when impostor syndrome and confidence gaps grow.

This fear was prescient for Tamara Warren, who pivoted from being a journalist who covered the Detroit automotive beat to launching a tech company for female car owners. Both careers were tied to the automotive industry, but otherwise the jump was stark. There is a big difference between being a journalist and being a founder-CEO. Tamara felt overwhelmed by the new skills she would need to learn. As Tamara put it, "I was scared to have to go outside of my lane." Tamara wrote about the automotive business, but she had never worked in business. She

Afraid

worried that the skills gap was too wide and that she wouldn't succeed. She felt like an impostor trying to play the part of founder-CEO.

Women's tendency to experience impostor syndrome is well documented in research. The robust research dates to 1978, when two female academics published "The Imposter Phenomenon in High Achieving Women."[5] In their work as professors, the researchers encountered a perplexing reality. They worked with accomplished female students with the highest qualifications and pedigrees, and yet these women *still* believed they didn't deserve their success. "I saw these people who had gone to the best schools, often private schools, had highly educated parents and excellent standardized test scores, grades, and letters of recommendation . . . but here they were, saying things like, 'I'm afraid I'm going to flunk this exam.' 'Somehow the admissions committee made an error.'"[6]

Career changes are a breeding ground for impostor syndrome, as women are moving from a familiar, comfortable place to a new destination with challenges, unknowns, and uncertainty. But guess what? Career changing is inevitable in today's economy. Women cannot avoid change, even if they want to. The better strategy is to find a way to harness our fears and overcome our impostor feelings—to make the career changes we desire and deserve, despite our fears.

AFRAID OF A HIGHER BAR FOR WOMEN

It's critical to overcome fear. It's also critical to acknowledge that women's fears exist within corporate systems designed for men, systems that negatively bias women and women of color. Women are savvy. They know, sometimes consciously, other times subconsciously, that they may have to work twice as hard as their male counterparts. Their fear is rooted in reality. It's hard to navigate corporate environments and successfully make a career change when women have less access to relationships, role models, and capital and more responsibilities related to childcare, parental care, and home management.

Cary Lin knew this truth well. Cary worked in corporate roles before pivoting to become the cofounder and CEO of a sustainable beauty company. She grappled with knowing when it was the right time to take the jump, and in her calculus, she heavily weighted the gender bias she would face as a female cofounder of color. She understood the path would be harder for her. Cary laughed in our interview when she told me, "Men can wake up one day and think, *I've been a growth manager at a tech company, so I'm qualified to be the CEO of a beverage company.*" But she added, "Women, even if they have a lot of experience, often can't get away with that. The bar is higher."

Cary's concerns about starting a company and raising capital as a female cofounder of color are justified and real; in 2021, all-female founding teams raised just 2.3 percent of venture capital. The picture is even more dire for women of color, with Black and Latina female founders receiving *less than half a percentage* (0.43 percent) of venture capital in 2021. Women face bias in investor perception, with VCs preferencing funding pitches associated with male voices or images.[7] And the VC industry is made up largely of men—65 percent of VC firms don't have a single female investor. Across the board, women in positions to fund start-ups and "write checks" are few and far between—9 percent in 2018 and closer to 14 percent in 2021.[8]

This very real bias influenced the career choices Cary made on her path to becoming a cofounder. Cary is strategic. To prepare, she dedicated almost ten years to building the ideal founder resume, one that would make her as protected as possible in a highly biased VC/start-up world. As Cary described in our interview, "I wanted to feel confident and totally unassailable. If an investor was going to pass on me, I wanted to trust that it wouldn't be because of my background or my qualifications."

FEAR CAN LEAD YOU TO GOOD PLACES

One of the biggest challenges is that it's hard to know whether fear is guiding you to the right or wrong place.

Afraid

Fear has been a part of almost every career decision I've ever made. In some cases, it has led me to fantastic places. In others, I wish I could go back and tell my younger self, "Don't let that fear guide you." For example, when I was a college student approaching graduation, I was terrified that I didn't have a clear career path or plan in place. Because of this fear, I decided I needed to take some action, right or wrong. I applied to law school and was accepted. In the time between my acceptance and starting law school, I realized that basing a long-term career decision just for the sake of having a plan wasn't the smartest idea. I declined my acceptance and never went.

Then, when I was job hunting after college, I accepted the very first job I was offered, even when I was in the late interview stage with another company that I preferred. The other company was seeking to fill a role in recruiting and people management. It was an area I found very interesting, but at the time, the "people" function was still "HR"—and HR often got a bad reputation. I was afraid of what people would think if I went into a recruiting or people role. And I was afraid that my first job offer might be the only offer I would ever receive. So I dropped out of the application process and accepted the first offer. I look back now and think, *What was I so afraid of? Why didn't I go after the job that really interested me?*

And yet fear has also led me to make fantastic decisions for my career. After working for a few start-ups, I worried I didn't have enough "serious" business experience. I had only my liberal arts degree and scrappy start-up experience, but no formal business education or training. I felt like an impostor in the business world. And I let that fear push me toward applying for an MBA. Then, when I started my MBA, I was even more terrified. I thought I would be uncovered as a fraud. I expected my classmates and professors to judge my lack of experience with things like Microsoft Excel or economics. Thankfully, my fear of being unprepared in the business world was stronger than my fear of feeling like an admissions mistake. I let my first worry push me toward business school—but I didn't let my worries about fitting in keep me from going.

This pattern played out more and more in my career. Fear infused every decision. And I didn't have a framework for reflecting on whether that fear was pushing me in a direction that would help my career or was holding me back. My continued fear of not being ready enough for the business world is what motivated me to move into management consulting. Though I struggled to thrive in that role, it proved an advantageous move for my career. It taught me concrete skills like proficiency at Microsoft Excel and softer skills like resilience.

But then, when I knew it was time to move on from consulting, I let fear hold me back. When I was debating leaving consulting, I worked with a career coach for the first time. In one of the first exercises with my coach, I reviewed a list of alumni jobs and companies and circled the jobs that interested me. I highlighted a lot of jobs related to people operations, and even career coaching. But when my coach asked me about it, I panicked like a deer in headlights. I was afraid of admitting an interest in this area of business, one in which I had no experience and that many still judged as old-school HR, an outdated function that real businesspeople didn't want to pursue (a wildly inaccurate stereotype, but one that existed within management consulting circles). I look back now and think, *Why was I so afraid of what other people thought?*

MAKING YOUR FEAR WORK FOR YOU

Fear continues to be a part of every career decision I make. And that is true for many women, even those who operate in the highest-power circles. The most prominent, successful women we celebrate in the news share this experience of fear, but they actively work to harness it and make it work for them.

Sheryl Sandberg, former COO of Facebook, hesitated to join Google because she worried it was a step back in her career, pivoting from the Department of Treasury where she managed thousands of people to a no-name technology company called Google where she would manage a team of four. But the fear of taking a step back can make you stay in one place and never grow, and that's just as scary. As Sheryl reflects,

"There are so many times I've seen people not make that jump because they're afraid they'll . . . move backward."[9]

Ann Shoket, former editor-in-chief of *Seventeen*, recalls how terrifying it is to break away from a predictable career path. When Ann's father gifted her a copy of *Who Moved My Cheese?*, a cautionary tale of getting so stuck in your own routine that you can't find new cheese, Ann was unamused. She didn't want to find new cheese. She wanted a stable, secure career. Ann has written about the great fear that accompanies career changes; she describes career pivoting as a high-anxiety activity, just as bad as toxic bosses who make you cry or coworkers who sabotage and undermine you. The fear of career changing can be paralyzing. We imagine that total career failure is lurking out there waiting to find us—a quicksand trap we can easily fall into.[10]

But the women who are most successful, authentic, and joyful in their careers are the women who can move forward despite being afraid.

Sara Blakely, founder of Spanx and self-made billionaire, often talks about how overcoming your fear empowers you to step into new, often *bigger* opportunities. "I have realized as an entrepreneur that so many people don't pursue their idea because they were scared or afraid of what could happen. My dad taught me that failing simply just leads you to the next great thing."[11]

Women often say that what holds them back from a career is the tactical know-how of making a switch—things like tuning up their resume, preparing for interviews, or writing their own business plan. But in my research, the deeper truth is that women are fantastic at executing career pivots—once they are committed to going for them. The greater challenge is harnessing the emotions you need to move past in order to move forward.

Meredith Vieira, broadcast journalist and TV star, described this when asked about her career and the pivots she has made. Vieira describes the biggest barrier to career pivots as people's mindsets. "Changing careers or even pivoting within a career is risky. That's the thing that tends to keep us where we are. Once you get that piece cracked, the more practical part—the how do I apply my skills from one industry to another—that piece tends to flow automatically."[12] So how can you harness such a powerful emotion like fear? First, understand that being scared about making a change in your career is *normal and expected.* The definition of the word *pivot* itself sounds scary: "a pin, point, or short shaft on the end of which something . . . rotates or oscillates."[13] A pivot sounds technical, precise, precarious. *Do I really trust the one central point, pin, or shaft to which I'm chaining my entire career?* It's understandable that so many women feel afraid when they consider redefining their career trajectory.

But the good news is that you *can* redefine your relationship with fear. You can learn to harness fear rather than let it control you. Part of that process is to spend more time understanding your relationship with fear. It's important to acknowledge, redefine, and ask the basic question: Why are you so afraid of a career pivot in the first place? We must distinguish between the good fear that leads us to new challenges and experiences and the bad fear that really is just holding us back from something great. The stories included in the rest of this book will help show you how other women have moved past their fears to be open to new possibilities, prepare for their career evolution, and ultimately lean into them.

As a starting point, the following reflection exercise will help.

REFLECTION EXERCISE

1. What are you most afraid of when it comes to your career?
2. Which failure has helped you most in your career?
3. I know you spend time thinking about what would happen if your career shift wildly failed. But what might happen if your career shift wildly succeeds?

PART II

HOW TO EMBRACE...

CHAPTER 6

ROLE MODELS

INSPIRATION TO PIVOT

Women often consider a career pivot when they are inspired by someone else's career. When a woman sees someone with a career that she admires, she starts to think, *What would it take for me to do that?* Role models are so important in how women envision their career trajectory. In fact, many women I interviewed credit a role model for inspiring or guiding their pivot.

Role models that influence career pivots fall into two buckets: functional role models and inspirational role models. Functional role models are those who are in the precise position you want to be in; they have the C-level title you've dreamed about or started the type of business you aspire to. Since they have built a similar career path, they offer a tactical road map for how you can execute your pivot. On the other hand, inspirational role models might be doing something very different from your career interests. However, they have an *approach* to their career that is inspiring. Often these women are brave, bold, courageous—the way you want to be but aren't today.

Role models are critical for women throughout their careers, but *especially* when considering a career change. When you're making a pivot, there are so many unknowns about the career path you are embarking on. Identifying people in your network and community who can illuminate the path and make it easier to navigate is key to succeeding.

Most women know how important it is to have role models. Two-thirds of women believe it's highly important that women beginning their careers have more examples of women in leadership positions. And 82 percent of millennials wish there were more role models.[1] Women know from experience how much role models matter, and research confirms their personal experience. Studies show that role models do three things for people: they serve as models of behavior, they represent what's possible, and they inspire. The presence of role models can change behavior and make people more motivated, more committed to their goals, and more willing to set new ones.[2]

FUNCTIONAL ROLE MODELS

The presence of an influential role model came up in many of my interviews with women. Brooke Morrissey was fresh out of college when she started a job at a law firm. She wasn't passionate about corporate law, but it felt like the "right" kind of job to take. After eighteen months, she felt unhappy; her heart, brain, and energy told her this was not the right fit. But she also felt stuck. She had the idea that she wanted to shift to more purposeful work, something where she was helping others. She had learned about a nonprofit organization that hired live-in volunteers for six months. She wanted to do it but was worried about leaving her job. It wasn't common to take six months off to volunteer, especially early in your career. *There must be a reason no one else does this*, she thought. *Will it negatively affect my future career prospects? Will I not be able to get another job?*

The idea of volunteer work stayed in her mind, but always as a dream—something someone thinks about but never does. That changed when she reconnected with a childhood friend. As they caught up, Brooke learned that her friend had volunteered for the exact nonprofit Brooke had considered. The friend spent a year volunteering as a teacher and had recently returned to the United States to work a traditional corporate job. In this friend, Brooke found a functional role model. She saw someone who had done it—who had been where she wanted to be. Her friend provided a blueprint for how to take time off, volunteer, and return to the workforce successfully.

Running into her friend provided Brooke with the role model and blueprint that she needed. She was able to see that it was possible and realistic. When I asked Brooke whether she would have left her job and traveled halfway across the world to volunteer if she hadn't reconnected with her friend, her answer was simple: "No."

Having a functional role model can be a "make or break" for women when it comes to changing your career. Many women need a functional role model because they need the confidence to know that the step they are about to take has been tried and tested before. Women see that they are not the only ones who have desired a career change, and they are not the only ones to act on those desires and successfully pivot. Functional role models offer a road map for the journey. They guide us and provide a light to better see the path ahead.

Another example is Carrie Collins, who pivoted from a legal career to higher education administration with the dream of becoming a university president. Carrie knew there were gaps in her experience, but nonetheless she wanted to make it happen. She had seen another female university president at a networking conference and was inspired. *I'd like to be a university president like her one day*, Carrie thought. When Carrie saw the same university president months later at another networking event, she walked up to her and said, "I've been following you because I want to grow into a president role one day." Carrie and her role model now talk monthly, and Carrie's role model provides pragmatic advice for her progression toward a president position. Carrie is learning from her fairy god mentor (as she calls her) the tactical steps and blueprint to achieve her career goal of becoming a president. Not everyone will have such clear focus as Carrie did or as direct access to the ideal mentor. But we can all model Carrie's behavior, which is the act of leaning into the people who inspire you and staying open to learn from them.

INSPIRATIONAL ROLE MODELS

Sometimes role models do not have the exact career you are dreaming of, but they have an approach to career that is inspiring—and sometimes stops you in your tracks. Michelle Obama is a great example of someone who found an inspirational role model.

After starting her career as an attorney at a big law firm, Michelle grew unhappy. Yes, she had played by all the rules—but she wasn't winning. The idea that her carefully laid career path wasn't delivering the satisfaction she wanted was deeply unsettling. Her plan wasn't working, but how could she change? Then she met Barack Obama. Barack had a completely different outlook on career. Michelle saw her career as a linear, regimented process. On the other hand, Barack saw his career as a meandering river with infinite turns. He never expected his career to follow a straight line. Barack was equally successful—working at the same prestigious law firm as Michelle—but he also dabbled in public service and believed he would leave the law firm at some point.

Barack became an inspirational role model for Michelle by opening her eyes to a different way of approaching and building a career. Barack never struggled with whether he had the *right* to pursue a different career—a guilt that Michelle struggled with deeply. Barack instinctively followed his energy and interests, and he wasn't afraid to break a linear path or take a step back. This was transformative for Michelle. She had thought there was only one way to succeed—climbing the ladder in front of you—but Barack, a man with great talent, intelligence, and ambition, was showing her there was a different way. When it came to her career, "Barack Obama taught me how to swerve," says Michelle.[3]

Role Models

ROLE MODELS ARE EVERYWHERE—OR ARE THEY?

I have looked for role models in my career. But often I haven't found them. In my roles in corporate organizations, I looked up to leadership, but there was no clear role model. I wonder if it is because there have been so few women in leadership in the corporate organizations where I worked. There were always male leaders to look up to, but their leadership style (extraverted, loud, competitive) was often completely opposite to mine (listener, consensus-driven, cautious). And as I started to think about starting a family, it was clear that male leaders would not share the same burden of blending career and family life.

I always thought this was a "me" problem, but there's a reason I found it so hard to identify role models. Women do face barriers in finding role models, particularly within corporate environments, because women are underrepresented in leadership positions across most industries and companies. The obvious outcome: If you tend to identify with women leaders, there are simply fewer role models to choose from. This is a negative reinforcing cycle: With fewer role models, women are less likely to achieve the highest rungs of success, and therefore less likely to be future role models for the women behind them. And with men predominantly in leadership positions, our stereotypical definition of what it means to be a leader stays intact—as stereotypically male, rather than female, behaviors and attributes.[4]

For some women, role models easily appear in their life. For others, it takes luck and coincidence, but they find models. But for still others, role models never come. We hear loud and clear the importance of finding role models to succeed—but what should women do if the right role models just aren't out there?

One solution is to redefine your search from finding a single role model who encompasses all that you want—the right career path, in the right industry, with the same approach to balancing family life—and instead, look for an array of role models. Each individual role model might represent just *one* element of what a successful career or life looks like. Some refer to this approach as a "developmental network" or a "personal board of directors."[5] Each director on your board helps you advance, learn, and grow in a *specific* skill set. "Because careers today are so complex, we need multiple mentors—a personal board of directors or what academics call a *developmental network*."[6]

Shifting your focus from finding the one-stop-shop role model to building a personal board of directors can help you more effectively identify role models. This approach broadens the pool of candidates who could be the right role model for you, including male role models. In practice, this may mean modeling a male leader's ability to get access to C-level leadership—but not the way he manages his team. Or it might be a female leader's path taking on roles across multiple departments to gain varied experience—but not her final leadership role in marketing when you really want to be in finance.

In the next chapter, we talk about a stage of career pivots in which role models can play a big part: opening your mind to new career possibilities. In other words, you'll learn how to shift from a one-path mindset to being open to other off-ramps, pivots, and less-traveled paths.

Opening your mind to new possibilities can feel daunting. But you have examples in your life (or out in the broader world) that make those possibilities feel more real. Reflect on the models that inspire you most through the following reflection exercise.

REFLECTION EXERCISE

1. No filter: What did you love to do as a kid? What did you want to be when you grew up? Why?
2. Whose career do you admire most? Why?
3. What element do you most want to add to your career identity?

CHAPTER 7

NEW POSSIBILITIES

WE DON'T LIKE CHANGE

Many women are reluctant to consider new career paths. It is comfortable to stay in your comfort zone. It is comfortable to trust that if you *just check every box*, you will get exactly where you want to go. It is comfortable to keep your career identity the same. Taking a chance on a different path is scary, especially for women who have followed a traditional, prescribed career path and achieved success doing so. But keeping your eyes open to new career directions is what creates limitless potential. It can lead to bigger and better success, if only you let it. Who knows—you may become a C-level executive, record-breaking filmmaker, or elected congressional official. We can learn from examples of women making big career transitions to see the great outcomes that are possible. These women also show us *how* they let go of their fear to open and envision a new path.

Opening your mind to a new career path is particularly fascinating to me because it has been such a difficult concept for me to adopt in my own career journey—for example, writing this book. I started taking concrete action on this book after a decade in my career, when I finally realized that the fancy brand names on my resume everyone told me would bring satisfaction in reality were not satisfying me. But the roots of the book go back even further.

Growing up, I loved to read and write. I was a bookworm. I would hole up in my room, reading in my bed and looking out the window. As soon as I could write, I published my first books—a collection of sticky notes stapled together with a few words on each note. I was in my own literary world, and I loved it. But as I got older, I also got more self-conscious. Why did my siblings tease me for reading? Why didn't other kids like to write? I found other activities to fit in. But I still loved to read and write. In high school I enrolled in a creative writing course, telling people, "I'm taking it because it fits my schedule." *What was I so afraid of?* I still remember to this day some of the essays I wrote in that creative writing class. I can't say the same about any other high school class.

In college I chose my major mostly because students were required to write a thesis. I studied representations of women and mothers in media and pop culture, showing the double bind that makes it impossible for women to be perceived as good moms and good career women at the same time. In my MBA program, I led the first-ever research study analyzing the participation rates of female and male students to prove my hypothesis that women participated less in quantitative classes.

My passions are clear: writing and advancing women. But in 2020, when I received an invitation to participate in a course to learn how to write a book, my immediate reaction was "What does this have to do with me?" I was a businessperson a decade into my career, not a book person. So I said no. That "no" stayed in my brain and heart and started to nag me. It was like an annoying sibling poking me every few days. "Why did you say no? Why did you say no?"

I simply could not open my eyes to writing this book. I would not consider that I *might not be a traditional businessperson*. I had a plan and a track, and I was desperate to stick to it. I didn't start my book writing journey until I became pregnant with my daughter. Becoming a new mom gave me the courage to reconsider my career identity and think about doing things differently. I finally did something with my research and began writing. I was motivated by my hopes and dreams for my daughter. When I looked at my daughter, above all else I wanted her to feel comfortable in her own skin and to be whoever she wants to be. When I looked in the mirror, I realized I wasn't who I wanted to be when it came to my career.

It was time to open my eyes to something new.

BUT SOMETIMES WE MUST

So many women I interviewed start their careers in the comfort zone of a fixed, structured career vision. Susan Aminoff had dreamed of working in advertising since she was sixteen years old. When she entered the workforce, she knew exactly where she was headed. "I was one of the lucky ones that knew what I wanted to do since I was a kid. I went to school for it, and then I dove into climbing the ladder," recalled Susan.

Susan spent more than a decade thriving in the advertising world. She worked in an agency providing services to her clients. One client trusted her so much that they began to expand her scope of work. No longer doing just advertising, she was also doing companywide strategy meetings and attending every executive meeting. This broader scope of work was exciting for Susan. But it also brought to light an uncomfortable reality. Susan—who had always believed she wanted to build a career in advertising—was now acknowledging that a much bigger world existed out there.

Susan was no longer just the brand person or the marketing person. She now was taking on bigger business responsibilities. For many people this would be great—more opportunity! But for Susan it broke the course of the steady, reliable career ladder she had been climbing since she was sixteen. What did this mean for her carefully laid-out plans?

LEAP

Susan's identity as an advertising person was shaken up. "All of the sudden, I realized that I was thirty-three years old and had no idea what I would do with the rest of my life. I still had many years of work ahead of me, and I had no idea what I wanted to do with my life." Detached from the identity she had clung to for so long, Susan was anxious, but she also felt the freedom to explore. She encountered a career exploration exercise called the Seven Stories that helped her identify the parts of her work that were memorable and important. She got increasing clarity on the elements of work that really mattered: she liked to mentor people, and she liked to introduce new concepts. "I started seeing the threads of the tapestry that is me," reflected Susan, "different threads about myself that had been with me since I was two or three years old."

Susan loved her newfound freedom to reinvent her career identity, but it also came with challenges. Sticking in her comfort zone meant no rejection. Now that she was open to new doors, she experienced the pain of not always being able to walk right through those doors. She interviewed for a role at Starbucks and did not receive an offer after the final interview round. When she accepted a job at a different company, she expected a quick promotion but then felt disappointed and embarrassed when she never received that promotion.

In the moment, those failures were devastating. But today Susan sees them simply as turns in the road. "I started to have some agility and resiliency. I started realizing this doesn't mean my life is over. It just means I need to pivot." These pivots and redirections have shaped her career trajectory and moved Susan forward, often toward a better opportunity. For Susan, acceptance that her trajectory will not be linear is a mindset shift that cannot be overstated. As Susan recalls, "This was a tectonic-level shift in how I valued myself and what I'm capable of."

Susan is thankful that she opened her eyes to career opportunities broader than what she planned as a sixteen-year-old going into advertising. "I feel so lucky that I lost my identity at thirty-three," she explained. "That was frightening and really scary. It hit me like a ton of bricks. But man, I learned it early, and I've had a fabulous career because of it. My life has flourished in ways I could never have imagined because I've been receptive and open to shifting my identity and accepting whatever comes next. I chose to see that I'm in charge of my own tapestry and the threads can be made up of whatever I want. If I decide I want red instead of green, I'm not going to apologize for that."

A STRAIGHT LINE ISN'T THE ONLY WAY TO GET THERE

Many of the most successful women that we see today—business leaders, politicians, creatives—reached the height of their success after a major career change. A straight line is not the only way to get there.

Ava DuVernay is a famous director, producer, and screenwriter. She is behind mega movies like *A Wrinkle in Time* (with a $100 million budget), historical dramas like *Selma* starring Oprah, and powerful, award-winning documentaries like *13th*. But what many don't know is that DuVernay's film career was launched only after a big pivot midway through her career. DuVernay started her career in journalism and public relations. It wasn't until she was thirty-two years old that she even picked up her first camera.[1]

In 2008 she created her first documentary, *This Is Life*, about the hip-hop scene at a local cafe. Two years later she followed up with her first feature film, *I Will Follow*, and finally acknowledged that telling important stories through film was the work she wanted to do. And so, at thirty-five, Ava considered the possibility that filmmaking would be her new career direction.

Ava sees her story as proof that any woman can shift her career identity and open her mind to climbing a different ladder. "For me to pick up a camera as a Black woman who did not go to film school—this is a testament that whatever path you're on right now is not necessarily the path you have to stay on," Ava has said.[2] If you are on a path that you know is not the right path for you, you have a choice. You can pivot. This is true regardless of your race, age, or any other factor you see as limiting. There is always the option to put one step in front of the other—in a different direction. Success may not come overnight. But that one step pivots your direction and begins the path of moving forward to reach new goals.

Alexandria Ocasio-Cortez shot into the public's view in 2018 when she won the Democratic primary in New York's 14th congressional district. Part of why Alexandria catapulted into the public eye was her story. Before her campaign run, she worked as a bartender and community organizer. How could a bartender win a congressional district seat? Joy Behar put it bluntly when Alexandria visited *The View* in June 2018: "Your win sent shock waves, basically, through the Democratic Party. They did not expect it."[3]

But Alexandria was motivated—and open—to the possibility that she *could* be a congresswoman. She believed she had the right to envision that path. Her motivation was simple: "I felt like we could do better and that we could be better as a country. We hadn't had a primary election in 14 years in New York—14. So it was clear that no one else was going to be doing this work. And I figured, you know what, if no one else was going to do it, and if I feel like we can be better, then that means it's my responsibility to do something."[4]

HOW TO OPEN YOUR EYES

So how can women embrace this mindset and believe they have options and the power to pivot? The first step is to demystify what a career pivot looks like. Ava DuVernay and Alexandria Ocasio-Cortez are exceptional examples of career changers. For most women, their paths feel out of reach. But the reality is that career changes are highly common. As previously noted, people change jobs an average of twelve times in their careers. And millennials change jobs three times more often than other demographics.[5] A successful pivot does not require that you become an elected official or famous movie director. It is not a move reserved for the "special" people with "special" resources. *Everyone, everywhere, is pivoting.*

The second step is to recognize your fear. Pivoting your career, particularly if you've been on a steady track over the long term, is terrifying! In fact, on the scale of stressful events, changing your line of work ranks just below the death of a close friend.[6] Women try to mask this fear with rationale, coming up with "practical reasons" for why they can't pursue what they really want in their careers. *I don't have the right skill set. My job is good enough. No one would hire me.* But as Jim Carrey told college graduates in a 2014 commencement speech, "So many of us choose our path out of fear disguised as practicality."[7] Instead of facing fear head-on, we come up with excuses that are easy to accept. *Don't choose the trajectory of your career based on fear.*

The third step is giving yourself permission to make mistakes. Your entire career trajectory does not depend entirely on mastering the immediate pivot in front of you. If you make a mistake during your pivot, you'll have on average eleven more chances to get it right. *Pivots are inevitable, so take the pressure off getting it perfectly right this one time.*

It takes role models, reflection, and sometimes luck for women to open their minds to new career possibilities. Susan's plan was to climb a steady advertising ladder, but a combination of opportunity and failure set her on a different path. She learned that she had the capacity to define her own career and step outside the professional identity she had once clung to. Ava explored her interest in filmmaking, despite being thirty-two years old with no camera experience. Alexandria believed that no path is too crazy, even the pivot from bartender to elected congressional official.

And I was able to open my eyes to a new career path too. I finally faced up to my fears. I hadn't turned down writing a book because I didn't want to. I turned down writing a book because it was *exactly what I wanted*—and sometimes, that's the scariest.

Good things come when women stay open to opportunities. In the next chapter, we see that career changes don't need to be viewed only as a risk to your career success. In fact, for many women, their career pivots are what launched them to even bigger and better success on both a personal and a professional level. But first, reflect on the new career possibilities that are available to you today.

> **REFLECTION EXERCISE**
>
> 1. What unexpected event has most positively affected your career?
> 2. Up until now, what rules have governed your career? What's one rule you want to get rid of? What rule will you replace it with?
> 3. What are five career opportunities you would immediately say yes to if they presented themselves?

CHAPTER 8

RISKS

THE REWARDS-OBSESSED MINDSET

Many women approach career transitions with a risk-based mindset. They think about what they stand to lose. *If I switch my career path, what will I lose out on? What will I give up?* Women worry that they won't like their new direction. They worry that they will make less money. They worry that others will judge them. They worry that they will fail. There are many flavors of these worries, but all of them are fundamentally the same—they worry that making the change is *risky*, that *bad things will come*.

In my own career, I have been the poster child for this risk-based mindset. I evaluated all my major career decisions based on risk. I struggled to leave a prestigious consulting firm because I worried that I would fail without a brand name on my resume. Many times I took the first job offer I received because I worried that I would not receive another. Even when I did make changes and moved to new companies or roles, I still struggled to view them optimistically. I never thought about the rewards they would offer. I only thought about the risks they would reduce: *My burnout won't be as bad; I probably won't make more money elsewhere; the clients won't be as demanding; I'm unhappy where I am, so I don't have a choice.* These assessments of opportunity are all rooted in negativity. Why couldn't I muster any optimism?

This negative, risk-based mindset about career changes is very limiting. One of the most critical things women can do to get more comfortable with a career pivot is to actively work to change this mindset. Women need to shift from a risk-obsessed mindset to a rewards-obsessed mindset. Instead of worrying about what they stand to lose—*What am I giving up by making a change?*—women need to consider what they stand to gain. There are so many possibilities of rewards: *I will love my job. I will make* more *money. I will become a subject matter expert. I will build a powerful professional brand that sets me apart from others. I will stay in the workforce longer. I will have flexibility to care for my family.*

Anytime you find yourself asking, "What if this wildly fails? What if this doesn't work?," actively shift your mindset. Take those same questions and flip them. "What if this wildly succeeds?" As Claire Krawsczyn, one of the small business entrepreneurs I interviewed, described, "We have a lot of thoughts that we don't necessarily need to believe. And once we realize that a thought is just a thought, we can create a new one."

A rewards-obsessed mindset is beneficial to making career pivots. Not only that, but refusing to take risks will limit and be detrimental to your career trajectory.

PLAYING BIG

Across the successful career changers I interviewed, one of the most important characteristics is the ability to think positively—to think big. Women who can transition from a risk-obsessed mindset to a rewards-obsessed mindset have a leg up when it comes to career transitions. They can think optimistically and see the bigger rewards that can come from going "off track" in their career path.

Risks

Take another woman I interviewed, Grace (who preferred to use a pseudonym in relation to her story). Grace built her career in financial services, including almost a decade at a top multinational investment firm. After graduating from business school, Grace returned to her former employer and progressed through a series of promotions, ultimately becoming the founder and head of innovation, responsible for launching new ventures that explored the unknown and placed strategic bets for future growth. In many ways, Grace had "made it." This was a dream job. She managed a large team, she was responsible for what she believed were the coolest parts of the business, and she got to think about fascinating topics such as the future of money, globalization, and disruptive business models.

But three years into her role, Grace felt ready to move on. She told family and friends she was considering leaving. They were shocked. "You are crazy!" "You are foolish!" "You are the head of innovation at a Fortune 100 company!" "You have your own P&L, team, staff!" "You get to be an intrapreneur, and you have huge projects underway!" "You have healthy paychecks!" "What is wrong with you? This is as good as it gets."

No one understood how Grace could consider leaving a gig that was so good. But Grace had a rewards-based mindset. She wasn't thinking about what she was going to leave behind. She was thinking about what she would gain moving forward. Grace wanted to be a bigger fish in a bigger pond. She wanted to keep growing toward the next step in her career. She wanted to challenge herself to do more. As Grace told me, "Instead of saying, 'This is going to be hard and scary, so I need to brace myself,' I started saying, 'If it's not hard and scary, then I don't want to do it.'"

Grace always agreed with her friends and family that she had it good in her job. But she wanted it *great*. She was playing big, as the fantastic women's leadership coach Tara Mohr likes to say.[1] "I believe I deserve the best," Grace said. "But I haven't risked or gambled on myself enough. Now, I'm betting on myself to win."

RISK IS GOOD

Taking risk is an important part of career building, particularly for women. But women get stuck in the risk trap. We tend to overestimate the likelihood that *something bad will happen* if we take a chance in our career. We overly perseverate on the risks while not factoring in the potential rewards. We also exaggerate the consequences of what will happen if things do go wrong. We think about doomsday scenarios and assume we have zero power to intervene when consequences arise. In a corporate world that fosters confidence gaps, it's no surprise that women doubt themselves and underestimate their ability to cope with risk. As a result, women feel safest not moving. We stick with the status quo and persuade ourselves it's sensible to stay put, even if we are in a suboptimal situation.[2]

But the reality is this: Your suboptimal work situation is not going away without any action. You *must* change. If you are unhappy in your career, staying put will not fix it. And not only is staying put ineffective in improving your situation; staying put can also actively *hurt your career trajectory*. This is because risk is a critical ingredient in how both men and women grow and advance in their careers. Without risk, you will not advance.

A profile of thirty-four ultra-high-performing leaders—entrepreneurs, politicians, celebrities, and athletes—saw one common thread: all had taken significant risks in their career. These leaders *actively* used risk to accelerate their growth. As the study showed, "Of the 34 people interviewed, all agreed that one constant anchored their calculations: the biggest risk was not taking one at all."[3]

For her book *Women Make Great Leaders*, author Jill Griffin also studied women and risk-taking. She saw similar findings that all the women in high-power careers had taken big risks at points in their careers. Her concern is that *not taking risks is a way to stagnate*. In one of my favorite lines from her book, Griffin writes, "Being risk-averse carries, well, risk." Not only does it prevent you from accelerating, but it can be viewed negatively in terms of leadership potential: "Risk-averse people often see themselves as deliberate, cautious, responsible, and thoughtful. Yet, others may see them as being reserved, lacking courage and belief in themselves, and less than inspirational—the very traits that can poison your ability to achieve more powerful roles in your career."[4]

The takeaway is that if you're not taking risks in your career, surprisingly, you might be creating more risk for yourself. And when people take leaps, they are generally more satisfied. In a fascinating study, *Freakonomics* author Steven Levitt surveyed twenty thousand people who were making major life decisions—something big, like quitting a job. The conclusion was straightforward: the people who took the leap were happier than those who didn't. This was regardless of the actual outcomes in terms of success, failure, or disruption to life. Now Steven holds this belief about risk-taking and change: "As a basic rule of thumb, I believe that people are too cautious when it comes to making a change."[5]

START THE MINDSET SHIFT

Shifting from a risk mindset to a reward mindset is not easy, especially for women who are comfortable checking boxes and sticking to a stable career path. When thinking of a career pivot, risk is the first thing that comes to mind. We are wired to overfocus on risk and underfocus on the reward.

However, it is very valuable for women to become rewards-obsessed when plotting their career journeys. When you are faced with decisions, your brain will automatically focus on the negative—the risks. To correct this, you should focus doubly on the rewards. Write out a list of five risks. Then write out a list of ten rewards. When you find yourself perseverating on what happens if it wildly fails, take a deep breath and ask yourself, "What happens if it wildly succeeds?"

Then remind yourself that you *need* to take risks. As we have learned from so many women, not taking a risk is often the biggest risk of all. Ask yourself, "By *not* pursuing this change, what amount of success (or happiness or flexibility or other reward) am I foregoing?" Focus on the rewards until the idea of staying becomes equally terrifying.

It is worth the work to get comfortable with risk. When women embrace a rewards-obsessed mindset, they see their full potential. They see the upside of their career trajectory. They gain confidence in their decision to make a change. They get excited about the opportunity to *bet on themselves*.

Answering the questions below will help you begin to get more comfortable with risk. Remember, sometimes the greatest risk of your career is taking no risk at all.

REFLECTION EXERCISE

1. What career risk has paid off most in your career?
2. How will not taking risks negatively affect your career?
3. What safety nets and support systems do you have (or can you build) to reduce your risk?

CHAPTER 9

YOUR SUPPORTERS

FIND YOUR SUPPORTERS

It is *not* simple to bet on yourself. When you are considering a career change, it is common to lack confidence. It is common to be afraid. It is common to not feel ready. This is especially true for women, and even more for women who feel they are making the jump alone. This is why support systems play such a critical role when it comes to women's career transitions. In many cases, women don't feel fully ready to reinvent their career until someone else helps show them they *are* ready or someone provides them with structural support to show them they *can* do it. Support systems are made up of different people playing different roles. There are spouses, professional mentors, personal mentors, business coaches, family, or a group of friends. The role of a support system is not just fluff; supporters play a critical role in helping women unlock their greatness and shift their mindset from "I don't know if I can do this" to "I will do this." They help women to be able to say, "I am ready." Supporters also provide women with pragmatic, tangible help to meet all the demands and needs in their lives.

More specifically, support systems play two important roles. First, the people in these systems remind you of your greatness—the skills, characteristics, and accomplishments you have built and accumulated. They build you up. They see the potential you may miss; they open your eyes to new possibilities. When your support system acknowledges and articulates your potential, this contributes to an important outcome: it helps you tap into your confidence and self-belief. This is critical for so many of us who are used to operating in work environments that make us question our ability.

But the second core role supporters play goes beyond emotional support. Supporters provide tactical, hands-on support. Careers are a big part of our lives—often one of our biggest responsibilities—but they are not the only responsibility. A full life presents obligations beyond just a career. Things like managing your health, or managing the health of loved ones, administrating a household, hands-on caring for parents or children, cooking meals, doing laundry—the list goes on. We need support systems because no individual can do it all. Our supporters must become our *literal* support.

But there is a trap when it comes to women and support systems: most often, women are raised to *be* the supporters rather than to *have* supporters. Setting up systems to *receive* support requires an active mindset shift and real work.

The path to each woman's support system and how difficult it is to cultivate varies. Some women have built-in support systems with a close-knit and supportive community. Others with limited community must get creative and build a network around them. No matter the circumstance, though, I argue that it is worth investing—sometimes *literally* investing—in a support system that can fuel the career that you want. Your career is the biggest financial asset of your life. Investing in it is not a luxury; it is a strategic decision.

Effectively engaging a support system is a powerful way to build the confidence and support you need to sustain your career success and execute any big career transition.

SUPPORTERS SEE WHAT YOU MIGHT NOT

When telling their career change stories, the women I interviewed frequently talked about one or two people who played a key role in supporting their career change. In my early interviews, I expected that these supporters helped the career changers in tactical, concrete ways. A mentor at work who made a key introduction. A friend in the industry who edited their resume. The spouse who did continual rounds of mock job interviews in the kitchen.

But the *real* support that women needed was not the pragmatic know-how of a career pivot. Instead, often the real support women needed was emotional support. The best supporters didn't help women to check another box by updating their resume. Instead, the best supporters helped women with a far greater task: convincing them to acknowledge and believe in their potential.

Let's take Claire Krawsczyn. In her early career, Claire was growing a successful career in public relations and communications. After relocating to a new city, Claire started working remotely, and with newfound flexibility and free time, she started building a side hustle. In addition to her full-time day job in PR, she took on freelance writing gigs. The freelance work gained traction quickly. Soon Claire was sacrificing her weekends and personal life to balance her day job and her side gig. She had to choose one or the other. Not a risk taker by nature, Claire leaned toward ending her side gig. She would stick with her full-time job, which also came with a full-time salary, benefits, stability, and security. Claire planned to shutter her side gig—until her husband had another idea.

Claire's husband, Adam, had a simple question: Why not drop the nine-to-five? Claire felt paralyzed by the risk. She struggled to justify how she could give up a stable career path for the opposite—no stability, no certainty, all risk. "For me the riskiest part was giving up all of the security that came with a really, really straightforward career path," recalled Claire. But Adam encouraged her to look at it another way. He believed the level of risk was much lower. Claire wasn't giving enough credit to herself and the traction she had achieved with her side gig. He reminded her that she had already built a book of clients and she was getting consistent referrals. "You've basically already built the business," he told her. Claire just needed more time to commit and grow it.

Adam helped Claire shift her mindset. Her side hustle deserved a little more respect. It was already a real business, with clients, an operating model, and an income that nearly matched her corporate salary. After more conversations, it clicked. Claire saw the potential that her husband saw in her, this time through her own eyes. "Looking back, I was surprised that I didn't see it myself. I almost cringe when I reflect that I didn't see it myself. I just never looked at it like that. It was encouraging and exciting." When I asked Claire if she would have pursued her business without her husband's support, her answer was no. And she believes that reality is rooted in being a woman and how we raise girls and women to understand what they deserve in their careers. Many women are most comfortable checking the boxes. And women are praised for checking boxes *in the service of others*. We sacrifice for our families, for our partners' careers, and to support our aging parents. But what we have never been encouraged to do is to sacrifice in service of ourselves. We are not used to putting things at risk for our *own* benefit. As a result, for many women, it takes having *somebody else* in your life see and fight for the potential that we don't always see or respond to on our own.

After more conversations, Claire and her husband made a decision: she would pursue the business full-time. They got to work to put together a business plan and were officially off to the races. A decade later and Claire is the owner and managing director of Verano Communications Group, an award-winning marketing and communications firm. She is also the cofounder of Cincinnati Spaces, which offers community space and meeting venues for entrepreneurs.

When reflecting on her decision to pursue her own business, Claire emphasized a piece of advice that helped her move from nervous hesitation to believing in herself and taking action. The advice? "Anytime you find yourself asking, 'What if this fails? What if it doesn't work?' also ask it from the positive lens. 'What if this *does* work? What if it blows up? What if this changes everything?' We have a lot of thoughts that we don't necessarily need to believe. And once we realize that a thought is just a thought, we can create a new one." Supporters help us create these new thoughts. They help us to see the potential that we may overlook on our own. And they fuel our belief and confidence that we can realize our career goals.

DEVELOPING CONFIDENCE IS CRITICAL FOR WOMEN

Claire's story brings up important questions on confidence. In hindsight, Claire acknowledges that she was extremely prepared to pursue her business full-time and that it offered even more potential than her traditional corporate career. After all, her side gig was producing the same income as her corporate job. This begs the question: Why couldn't she see the potential? Why did she need someone else to convince her that she was ready?

Unlocking confidence and self-belief is critical for women, who have to navigate the dynamic of confidence at work. Corporate working environments have not typically fostered confidence in women. One of the seminal pieces on women and confidence at work is from authors Katty Kay and Claire Shipman, who explored the topic in their 2009 book *Womenomics*.[1] Their research shows that women have the same levels of competence as men, yet they feel less self-assured, which can have negative impacts on their success. The original research was borne out of Katty and Claire's observations about their personal lives and careers. They were just like the women they studied: despite being highly accomplished and competent researchers and academics, both authors lacked confidence.

As they wrote in an article titled "The Confidence Gap," "Katty got a degree from a top university, speaks several languages, and yet had spent her life convinced that she just wasn't intelligent enough to compete for the most-prestigious jobs in journalism." Coauthor

Claire recognized the absurdity of Katty's lack of confidence, but when it came to herself, she suffered the same delusion: "Claire found that implausible, laughable really, and yet she had a habit of telling people she was 'just lucky'—in the right place at the right time—when asked how she became a CNN correspondent in Moscow while still in her twenties."[2]

In their research, Katty and Claire find evidence of this confidence phenomenon everywhere, even among the *most* accomplished female leaders across many industries. For example, All-Star Women's National Basketball Association (WNBA) player Monique Currie talked about how her male counterparts—even the male players who rode the bench and even the player who was the fifteenth of fifteen players on the roster—had superstar confidence that few women basketball players and athletes had. Technology entrepreneur Clara Shih, who joined the board of Starbucks before she was even thirty years old, described feeling like an impostor. Even Sheryl Sandberg, former COO of Facebook and best-selling author of *Lean In*, shares with Katty and Claire that many times she woke up feeling like a fraud.[3]

Other research confirms Katty and Claire's hypothesis that women have a harder time embracing confidence and belief in their potential. Female managers report more self-doubt about their job performance and careers.[4] Male business school students negotiate and ask for more money than their female counterparts.[5] A well-known analysis of personnel records at Hewlett Packard showed that women applied for a promotion only when they met 100 percent of the job qualifications, whereas men applied when they met 60 percent of the qualifications.[6]

It's easy to take Claire and Katty's research and say, "This is a simple problem with a simple solution." And indeed, many leaders—usually male leaders—responded to Claire and Katty with a flawed response: "Just be more confident!" But we know that women's self-perception does not relate to their competence.[7] When women are just as qualified and competent but not exhibiting the same level of confidence as men, we must look deeper. What's making women feel this way?

This isn't a problem with women. This is a problem with a dominant work culture that doesn't give women the *permission* to be confident—a work culture in which the rules of confidence and belonging are different, depending on who is playing the game. Ruchika Tulshyan and Jodi-Ann Burey, two experts on race, gender, and work, break this down in their excellent thought leadership on impostor syndrome. They beautifully describe the way it goes: "The same systems that reward confidence in male leaders, even if they're incompetent, punish white women for lacking confidence, women of color for showing too much of it, and all women for demonstrating it in a way that's deemed unacceptable."[8] Women won't win just by "being more confident." In fact, many women might be punished even further. So the answer is not to fix individual women. The answer is to fix the work environment that sets up women to fail when it comes to feeling empowered, confident, and capable at work.

But while we wait and fight for the system to change, we need strategies to cope. And support systems play an important role in coping. Our supporters can help see our potential. Having a support system becomes a strategy to counteract feelings of impostor syndrome, to think optimistically about your potential, and to embrace your potential and confidence in reaching your goals.

SUPPORTERS HELP US MAKE SPACE FOR CAREERS

Support systems are not only about changing your mindset. Support systems are also about making your career—and the career changes or reinventions you want—realistic to execute on a very pragmatic level. Careers are a big component of modern life, but our lives must have space to fulfill obligations outside of work. And ideally, we have space not just for life's obligations, but also for life's joys.

However, when it comes to prioritizing and claiming this space, the rules are different for women. Even at work, women are expected to play the support role. Here are two quintessential examples of this:

- In your meetings, who takes and distributes meeting notes?

- In your office, who plans team celebrations or buys farewell gifts for departing employees?

These types of expectations to support extend outside of the office. Women, compared to their brothers or male peers, spend more than twice the time caring for aging parents.[9]

A similar, stark difference appears when we look at working moms who are partnered with men. Despite living with their male partner in the *exact same* household with the *exact same* support and caretaking demands, women are more likely to take on the "second shift" at home and perform an unequal amount of household and childcare labor.[10] For working mothers without partners, there is simply no split at all.

High-success careers require high-level support. In a recent survey of more than 250 highly successful women, when asked, "How do you do it?" nearly half of the women surveyed responded, "Support from my spouse or life-partner."[11] Betsy Myers, director of the Center for Women and Business at Bentley University, runs global workshops on women's leadership, and she hears the same message from hundreds of women: some version of "I couldn't have gotten here without my incredibly supportive partner."[12]

But support like this is rare. The majority of women in the workforce are unmarried.[13] And even for women who *are* married, having a partner does not mean you have a partnership. There is more equity and more reciprocal support between partners in same-sex relationships and marriages. But for women partnered with men, the support is not there—in almost every scenario. First, female leaders are more likely to be in a dual-career household, whereas for men it is more common to have a stay-at-home spouse. Even in a single-career household where the male partner does not work outside the home, women *still* spend more time on household labor. This dynamic is *exacerbated* when women operate as the primary breadwinner in their household.

The more that men rely financially on their female spouses, the *less* household labor those men do. And all these scenarios prove to be the opposite for men: men benefit more frequently from a female partner solely dedicated to labor inside the home, men do less work inside the home no matter the working status of their spouse, and men who make more money outside the home do less labor at home.[14] *None of it makes sense.*

And for women in the United States, there is no structural support net to catch them. The United States is one of only six nations to *not* offer paid parental leave.[15] The cost of childcare in the United States is astronomical. For 80 percent of families, childcare exceeds the recommended affordability level set by the Department of Health and Human Services.[16] Women bear the brunt of these support gaps. Women are more than three times as likely as men to cite childcare availability or expenses as their reason for leaving the workforce.[17] And women are more likely to report that their childcare responsibilities hold them back professionally.[18] Our society asks so much of working moms and yet provides them with so very little. As the Marshall Plan for Moms writes, "Other countries have social safety nets. America has moms."[19]

YOU CAN'T DO IT ALL, AND YET YOU ARE EXPECTED TO

We don't need research to know this reality. *We live it.* We understand, through experience, that the question of being ready for a career change is not always so simple. The inequity we face when it comes to household labor, caretaking, and childcare is even more reason that we must be intentional and strategic when it comes to building our support system.

If you go with the flow, you will likely build a status quo operating system. And the status quo operating system is one of deep inequity that sets women up to fail. But you *can* purposefully build an operating system that sets you up for more success. You can invest in the support you need to pursue a full career. Or you can fight for more equity within your life. For example, new systems like Eve Rodsky's *Fair Play* are offering ways for partners and spouses to reimagine the division of labor at home and create more equity.[20] But it takes investment and a proactive strategy to implement more equitable systems for yourself and the people you support—and hopefully who support you in return.

While confidence and gender equity create challenges for women, they are not individual women's problems—they are *systems* problems. But if you're a woman at work, you know that you can't wait for the systems to fix themselves. In the meantime, you must develop coping strategies to exist, survive, and ideally thrive at work. And having a team of supporters is an important part of your strategy. When you're building your support system, there are a few elements to consider. The first is developing an investment mindset when it comes to your career.

In almost all cases, your career is the biggest financial asset of your life. When we think of financial assets, we know that we need to invest in them. It takes money to make money. But do you have this mindset when it comes to your career? Are you willing to invest in yourself and your career to fuel your success? It starts with investment—mental investment, but also real dollars. This could mean hiring an executive coach or a business coach to accelerate your success. It might be paying for an online course or finishing a degree. It could be hiring a babysitter to watch your kids after school ends.

The less support or financial security we have, the harder these decisions can be to make and execute. We all have limits and realities. But what I want to ensure is that we are not making decisions against our career simply because we lack an investment mindset. I love Rachel Rodgers's book *We Should All Be Millionaires* and her philosophy on work and making money for women of color (and all women). Rachel talks about how women are raised to view making money and investing in our career as selfish or greedy. But in reality, these are *revolutionary* acts for women that not only fuel their careers and their financial stability but also bring the economy into balance and create a more equitable world for all.[21]

Support systems at work matter too. Though typical work and corporate environments need dramatic change to set women up for success, it doesn't mean you should throw your hands up and give up. There are strategies and tools within your control that can help you to succeed more at work. And relationships are key.

The most common work relationship advice women receive is to find a mentor. But as you think about your support system at work, think about building a personal board of directors. Finding *a single* mentor who is your perfect career guide is like finding a unicorn. So many women go on a never-ending hunt that leaves them frustrated and feeling like they failed. *I can't find the perfect mentor who will change my career*, they think. Building a personal board of directors is more achievable. It's also more effective.

A board of directors should include mentors, yes. But it should also include sponsors and ambassadors. Sponsors act like mentors but also *sponsor* you; they open doors and create opportunity for you. They bring you into important projects, influence promotions, and push you ahead on your career path. They are your ears and voice in the rooms you don't yet have access to. Ambassadors are the people, at any level in your organization, who love you. They talk about you, hype you up—sometimes without even knowing it—and elevate your brand to other people throughout your work environment. When you build a personal board of directors, you acknowledge that there are many people who can play a role in advancing your career. And you get a bigger network, broader influence, and more support.

ACKNOWLEDGE THE SYSTEM AND INVEST IN IT TO MAKE IT WORK

The rules of the game are different for women and men navigating their careers. Even when women are overqualified and overprepared—even when they are perfect or *practically* perfect—many women still don't embrace their full potential. Women still lack or hide confidence. This is because the system has trained women to do this! White women are told to speak up more. Black women are told to speak up less. I want women to take those rules and rewrite them. Recognize that it is not *you* who needs fixing—it is the system that needs repair. Do you feel consistently insecure at work? Understand why *the rules* make it that way. Are you unable to bring your full self and opinions to your office? That's not a knock on *you*; it's a knock on the system. When you start to understand and acknowledge the flaws in the system, you'll start to reclaim some of the confidence that you've always deserved.

The rules are different at home too. Confidence aside, there is the challenge of leaning into a career change while balancing a personal and family life that asks a disproportionate amount from women. When it comes to work and equal partnership at home, there is no simple solution. Ambitious women are looking for true partners in building careers and caring for families. But at the same time, spouses—especially male spouses—expect their careers to take priority. What do we do? The women I interviewed for this book all made different decisions and trade-offs for their career. But no matter how different, each of their stories is worth celebrating. And so is your story and your choices. The important part is defining success for you—on your own terms.

But if you're stuck in a rut, if you're not feeling confident, and if you're feeling overwhelmed at home, the cause is not lost. Sometimes that lack of confidence can spark an intense drive to fastidiously prepare for your next career chapter. We explore what that looks like—and the good and bad that it brings—in the next chapter.

For now let's dive into that support system around you and the confidence you do (or don't) have when it comes to your career trajectory.

Your Supporters

REFLECTION EXERCISE

1. What is a moment in your career when you've thought, *I'm great at what I do?*
2. Who are your biggest career cheerleaders? What do they say are your strengths?
3. How would more confidence change the way you navigate your career?
4. What daily habit could you introduce to drive more free time at home?

CHAPTER 10

THE TEST-AND-LEARN APPROACH

WHAT WE *THINK* A CAREER PIVOT LOOKS LIKE

We often view career pivots through a Hollywood lens. We think that career pivots are the result of a dramatic, usually spontaneous, decision to say goodbye to corporate doldrums in favor of a richer and more glamorous life. The Hollywood story goes like this: After a particularly bad Friday at work, you march into your boss's office and abruptly quit. You walk out of your office building to a glorious weekend—you are finally free. The next day you are wandering around your neighborhood shops and notice a coffee shop for sale. *I'll become a baker*, you think. The scene ends and flashes forward. You are in a corner bakery, an adorable shop that you now own, and you are thriving in a blissful life where you are living your dream.

This story is simply not real. First, it's not real in that even if it *were* real, it wouldn't look like the Hollywood depiction. You are now the owner of a shop, but we never saw you working through the mortgage. You are now a baker, but we never saw you go through cooking school or take on entry-level roles where you arrive at work at 4:00 a.m. to prepare morning pastries. Even if you truly become a baker, your career pivot doesn't look like the above.

But this story is not real for a second reason. Generally, this is not how any woman makes a career pivot. This story simply doesn't happen. While a spontaneous and dramatic career pivot is exciting to think about, it's not how career pivots play out in real life, especially for women. Women are maniacal when it comes to preparation. Most career pivots are executed over a long period of time—we're talking multiple years—through a series of small, intentional steps.

This is good news for a lot of women who are not impulsive risk takers. What we see in real life—a methodical, measured approach to a career pivot—means that career pivots are accessible to everyone. Even the most conservative or cautious of women can adopt a test-and-learn approach that allows them to create change at their own pace without taking on significant levels of risk or uncertainty.

THE TEST-AND-LEARN APPROACH

My career change is an example of a "slow burn" career pivot, common for so many women. This book itself is the product of a test-and-learn approach to career change. After I had my first child, I knew I wanted a career change. I wanted research and writing to be a part of my future career. And I wanted to pursue a broader mission of helping more women succeed in their careers and their lives. For the first time in my career, I knew a lot about what authentically interested me in a career path. But that doesn't mean I was ready to suddenly quit my job. The opposite. My first thought was *I need to test my hypothesis*. Would I really enjoy research and writing? Would I be any good at it? Could I turn this into a viable job that provided an income?

Embarking on this book project while maintaining my full-time job was a way to answer some of these questions. Taking a test-and-learn approach allowed me to reduce the risk of writing a book. It didn't require that I risk my income or existing career up front. I didn't need to make an all-or-nothing decision, which is a good thing because I don't know that I would have been ready to take that plunge on day one. A test-and-learn approach also lowered the bar for starting the book. I was able to treat it as an experiment, which made it easier to commit. Moving forward with the project required only the hypothesis that this is where I wanted to move my career. It didn't require absolute certainty. Certainty would come later, after I had tested my writing and learned from my experience. And finally, writing this book is a catalyst for developing the skills and experiences I will need when I do make a more permanent pivot or transition. Before writing this book, would my career experience have qualified me to identify myself as an author? Not at all. But after testing and learning as an author through this book, do I have the right to confidently position my writing and book publishing experience? Unequivocally.

TEST AND LEARN YOUR WAY INTO A CAREER CHANGE

It's easy to romanticize the notion of a career change. We envision that career-changing women wake up one day with an unbridled passion and a full commitment to a new career. That calling is so strong that they immediately quit their current work and dive into their next career chapter. It's the Hollywood story again. But this rarely—*rarely*—is what a career pivot looks like. Nearly all the women I interviewed for this book approached career changes from a highly strategic perspective—with discipline and a structured approach that launched them toward the next phase of their career over time. Women take small steps to begin their transition and prepare over time. Women start by testing and learning.

For example, Kate Bennett left a career in management consulting to work in MBA Admissions at Harvard Business School. On the surface that looked like a pretty big change. A transition from strategy consulting with big corporations to working with students in a university setting? That is not a common transition for people leaving management consulting careers. But for those who had followed Kate's career closely, they knew Kate took many intentional steps to test, prepare for, and ultimately execute this transition.

Kate started in consulting to learn about business and keep her career options open. But from the start, she thought she might end up in education; she was inspired by her mom, who was a teacher. When Kate went back to business school and had a summer internship, she spent half of her summer working for a charter school. When she saw the impact she could have in education, she decided it was the right industry for her. The next summer she did another internship in education, but this time in a public school district. When her MBA program ended, Kate still wasn't ready to jump into education. She returned to her consulting role to continue on the steep learning curve, as well as get her tuition paid for through a sponsorship program where consulting firms cover tuition if the employee returns to work post-MBA.

Back at the consulting firm, Kate resumed client work. But she also had the opportunity to explore another type of work: managing the firm's entry-level talent, a group of recent college graduates who were starting their first jobs. She first tested this work in a project managing the consulting firm's summer internship program. It turned out that she loved it, so Kate wanted to test it further. After managing the summer internship program, she continued to work with this group by overseeing the recruiting process for college graduates moving into entry-level roles at the firm. Through these experiences, it became clear that Kate had a passion for managing talent and working with people in the early stage of their career.

Kate's test-and-learn approach was intentional. It prepared her for the ultimate career pivot—leaving consulting and going to work for a business school—by removing a lot of the risks and fears associated with a big change. As Kate recalled, "I think having a test-and-learn approach can be really effective. I was risk-averse, so as I approached this change, I tried to test and learn as much as possible. That way, when it came time to make the full jump, I really knew what I wanted to do."

Kate believes that testing out new career paths is a key part of anyone's career trajectory. This is particularly true for young professionals like those she worked with in consulting and while recruiting candidates at Harvard Business School. Why is testing and learning so important? Kate believes that it dispels the myth of a "single passion" and helps people to identify where they want to go and be confident in that direction. The number of people who discover early on in their careers exactly what they want to do is exceedingly low, although it does happen for some. What is more typical is that people have a directional sense when it comes to their career—a broad area of interest, a few certainties of *I don't want that*, and some ideas about what they might enjoy. When you are still playing around with your career goals, it becomes important to find ways to test your hypotheses. As Kate describes, this is where people can get strategic about projects or internships to get that data, test out a career, and *really* know what it's like before making a major jump without visibility.

A TEST-AND-LEARN APPROACH IS EVERYWHERE

When we look at prominent women who are at the top of their game, it can seem as though their success came overnight. But almost always, behind these women are similar stories of taking small steps toward their career success, with an eye to testing and learning along the way.

Earlier I referenced Ava DuVernay, one of today's most celebrated filmmakers. But Ava's career in filmmaking didn't start until she was more than a decade into a career in PR. When she finally picked up a camera at thirty-two years old, she didn't immediately leave her PR career behind. Her transition came with time. Though she knew she wanted to pivot into film, she laid a careful transition plan to make it a reality. As Ava described in a 2019 interview with *Variety* magazine, "I didn't want to stop my business while I tinkered in film when there was no precedent for a black woman being successful in film commercially at that time. . . . So I made my films on the side, and for my first five films I still worked my day job."[1] You read that right. Ava didn't consider a full career pivot until she was successful enough to be at the Sundance Film Festival.

If you live in or visit Boston, you might have heard of Joanne Chang. She is a successful chef, the owner of a series of bakeries and restaurants, and the winner of the James Beard Award for Outstanding Baker. But Joanne's career path and her pivot were slow and intentional—just like Kate's, Ava's, and many other women's paths. It started with a traditional business role after she graduated from college. In the "Hollywood" story, the next scene you see is Joanne becoming an award-winning baker and restaurant owner. It paints the picture that one day she quit the business world and the next day she was a celebrated chef.[2]

But the truth is that Chang had been laying breadcrumbs—no pun intended—for many years on her path to become an award-winning baker and restaurant owner. In college, Joanne started baking and selling chocolate chip cookies out of her dorm room.[3] Later, she developed a business plan on the side for a food company called "Joanne's Kitchen." And she also baked cakes and cookies for her coworkers.[4] Joanne's decision to forego her traditional business trajectory and instead apply to culinary positions was still a major pivot. But the notion that it came out of nowhere is a romanticized story. For *years* Joanne was honing her skills as an amateur baker and evaluating the business realities of becoming a restaurant and bakery owner. And then for many more years, she was training from the ground up in entry-level chef positions to earn her chops in the baking and culinary world.

Pivot: The Only Move That Matters Is Your Next One is a book dedicated to career pivots. In it, author Jenny Blake shares her own career pivot story. One of the major points she makes is that her career transition—leaving Google to start her own company as a career coach and author—was not overnight or out of the blue. Instead, she took an incremental approach that allowed her to fill in the gaps and prepare for her future career.[5]

The Test-and-Learn Approach

Jenny describes her pivot in a recorded *Talks at Google*: "If I had left Google to become a yoga teacher, that would have been a 180[-degree turn]. But instead, I was doing coaching and career development within Google, and I left to do coaching and career development on my own." While Jenny was working at Google, she completed coaching training during nights and weekends. Then, when a career development team was formalized at Google, she pivoted internally to join that team. Jenny's story shows that a pivot can be set up so that the gap you must leap over becomes smaller and smaller. You can build on your current professional experience and leverage what is already working.[6]

I also think of one woman I interviewed, Leela Srinivasan, the chief marketing officer of many tech companies, including the $40 billion company Checkout.com. Today Leela is a clear leader in marketing, but her career path wasn't always so clear-cut. Leela started her career off in what she described to me as a hodgepodge of jobs including things like *sales*. Sales was emphasized, almost like a dirty word, because at that point in Leela's career, none of her peers were in sales. But when she started recruiting for jobs after business school, her sales experience catapulted her to the top. Leela told me, "Recruiters were doing backflips over the fact that I had sales experience. Because sales and the skills you build as a salesperson—selling, negotiating, listening, tenacity, relationship-building—are really important." Her sales experience helped her get great job offers.

But it also showed Leela that testing and learning throughout your career, rather than committing to one fixed, permanent career path, can lead to some of your best outcomes. Because of her experience, Leela came to embrace the twists and turns of her career: "I stopped beating myself up for not taking the most direct, fastest path. Sure, sometimes there is a benefit to taking the fastest path. But you also miss out on the journey that builds different muscles and skills, and you don't know when those are going to be valuable. I am *much* better head of marketing because I did sales. I am *much* better because I spent time in consulting. So I stopped regretting the meandering."

TEST AND LEARN IS HERE TO STAY

Testing and learning is not only a good way to approach a career pivot; this approach is also the way that modern careers are unfolding today. An iterative career where you test, learn, adapt, and change simply reflects the realities of the modern workforce in which individuals frequently shift their career identity. The number of pivots can be even higher for millennials and Gen Z women who are still in the early or middle stages of their career progression.

We are used to thinking that the average career trajectory is like climbing a ladder. There is a linear path, and each step predictably leads you to the next rung. But today's careers are no longer like ladders. Today's careers are like a river. There are twists and turns, your career is affected by the world and environment around you—a global pandemic, for example—and you can't always see what's around the corner.[7] Learning to test and adapt your career, whether you're planning for a major pivot or not, is still a highly strategic skill to have as you navigate even the most straight and narrow of career paths.

One of the superpowers of career changers is that they learn to manage their career trajectory strategically and proactively. They learn to drop the traditional way we were taught to plan our careers, which is to plan and implement. We set a fixed, long-term goal and then build and implement a plan to reach that goal. A plan-and-implement approach works well when your career is like a ladder. You set your one constant goal (reach the top of the ladder), and you continually put one foot in front of the other to execute. But the test-and-learn approach that so many career changers adopt is *far* better-suited for today's careers. In a test-and-learn approach, you view career management as an *ongoing* development, one that is circular in nature because you are constantly testing, learning, and redirecting your career goals.

The book *Careers: An Organisational Perspective* offers a description of what career planning looks like in this approach, and it's something like this: an iterative process of reflection and action that leads to continued redefinition of career goals and possibilities based on leaps of insight or aha moments that you experience throughout your life and career. As those career goals and possibilities are updated, you are open to transitioning and adapting your career trajectory. Your career becomes fluid as you consistently test and adapt your journey.[8]

A test-and-learn approach to a career allows women to consider that they may not have a single passion, but instead that there may be many possible career selves they could evolve into. Unlike a ladder approach in which the goal is fixed, a career goal becomes fluid; you have permission to change.

I'M IN. HOW DO I START?

A test-and-learn approach can benefit women career changers in multiple ways. First, it is a way for women to address their fear of a career change. When you test and learn, you are gathering more information and new skill sets that lower the risk of your pivot; you know more about what you are getting into, and you are more prepared. Second, a test-and-learn approach to a career enables you to be wrong. This is so powerful that I need to repeat it: *a test-and-learn approach enables you to be wrong.* Your career goals are accepted as a hypothesis for where you want to go rather than a foregone conclusion. Third, and perhaps most important, testing and learning your way through your career is a way for you to gain the skills, network, and experiences necessary to succeed in your post-pivot career. Testing a new career—writing on the side, volunteering, starting with one or two clients in a side hustle—is a great way to build a foundation for a more permanent transition.

If testing and learning resonates with you, the first step is to develop that hypothesis for where you want to go. What do you want to do? This sounds simple, but repeatedly I hear women say, "I don't know what I want to do." But that's rarely true. I am here to tell you: *You know more than you are telling yourself.* You know what brings you energy, you know the work you naturally gravitate toward, and you know what you would do if you could maintain the same income but do any job in the world. The problem is not that you don't know. The problem is that you're not listening to what you know. Instead, you've been listening to the voices around you telling you what a good career looks like, maybe for a decade, two decades, or more. Your truths are buried deep down inside of you. Now you must do the work of unearthing those truths and reclaiming control of that knowledge.

This reflection is not fluffy. It's real, important work. You must think critically and honestly about your skills, your interests, and your values. You need to evaluate the work that you do today and what lights you up, even if it's only small pieces of your role. You need to articulate the work that you don't love doing. And most importantly, you must be brutally honest—even if the picture you paint is scary or unexpected. Look inside yourself and reflect. The answers are there. You just need to unlock them.

The reflection exercise below will help you begin to unlock this important knowledge. Then, in the next chapter, we explore how you can move from the test-and-learn phase to full execution. I talk about how to strategically prepare for your career pivot, while watching out for overpreparing and never taking the leap.

REFLECTION EXERCISE

1. What's one thing you can do this month to start moving your career in a new direction?
2. What are three elements you want to incorporate into your future career?
3. Earlier in your career, what assumptions or hypotheses did you have about work that proved to be wrong?
4. How will moving in incremental steps help your career development?

CHAPTER 11

PREPARING TO LEAP

THE INSTINCT TO PREPARE, PREPARE, PREPARE

It's easy to romanticize career pivots as impulsive overnight decisions. But my interviews paint a very different picture. Most women approach career pivots with a strategic, methodical, and meticulous process—including lengthy preparation over time. Our instinct as women is not to make swift decisions overnight. Instead, our instinct is to prepare, prepare, prepare. This preparation mindset can be valuable for career changes. As women, we have the discipline to diligently move forward on the path that leads us to our next step. At the same time, our desire to check every box before making a career pivot can slow us down. When we set the bar for preparation so high, our feeling of readiness—*Am I ready to leap?*—might never seem to come. More complicated is the fact that our inclination to diligently craft a bulletproof resume over time is for good reason. Women do face different expectations and biases than men when competing for a new career opportunity or pushing for an investment to launch their own business. The rules of the game are different depending on who you are. And if you're a woman or woman of color, the rules are tougher.

Preparation becomes a tactic—and sometimes a defense mechanism—as we play the game. The desire to be prepared played out across the first decade of my professional career. Right out of college, I stumbled into working in business roles for two start-ups where I felt completely *unprepared.* I found myself creating go-to-market plans for the business and leading relationships with major technology partners. I was in the business world but armed with no formal business education or training. I was constantly thinking, *I am not prepared to do this.* As a result, I became hyper-focused on building a bulletproof resume with the right experience that would make me feel like a "real" businessperson prepared to navigate her career. My end goal had nothing to do with finding the right career path for me. It had everything to do with filling in the gaps and weaknesses so that I could do my job.

In reality, *I was doing it.* Yet I felt wildly insecure. I had major impostor syndrome. I thought I was only making it because I was working in a small start-up. I told myself that if I moved to a big company, I wouldn't survive. I decided that I needed to be more prepared. I needed to check more boxes and get ready for a "real" business role. Enter business school. At that point, I didn't know many people who attended business school. But from what I could see, it seemed like the degree held a lot of cachet and gave people access to careers at prestigious companies. I went back to the thoughts in my head: *I don't have any real business experience. I need to show people that I have checked that business box.* That was enough reason for me.

I thought that two years of business school would make me feel prepared to go out into the business world. But as I started that second year, I still felt like I didn't know enough. My "get prepared" mission seemed far from complete. For that reason, I started to consider management consulting. Working in consulting, especially at one of the top three firms, McKinsey, BCG, and Bain, was the gold standard. People called it an MBA 2.0 because it offered another few years or more of business experience, this time working with the biggest clients in the world. Consulting terrified me, though. I felt a pit in my stomach. *I am going to feel overwhelmed and get swallowed up*, I would think. I was nervous to work seventy or eighty hours a week, which I knew wasn't out of the norm for consulting hours. I was nervous to constantly change industries and teams and clients, never settling into a routine. I wanted to live at home, not out of a hotel. I wanted to see my husband, my friends, my family. My heart was asking me, *What am I doing this for?* But my insecurity around my preparation was stronger. *I am doing this because I am still not ready.*

That fear around preparation rang loudest. So, when I received an offer from one of those consulting firms, I felt two emotions. First, I felt proud. I knew this was a job that many wanted, and I was one of the few who got it. *Maybe this means I do have something to offer*, I dared to think. But the second emotion was the opposite; it was that pit in my stomach—a mix of apathy and fear. *Other people want this job, but do I? And what is this pit in my stomach warning me about?*

WHEN IS ENOUGH ENOUGH?

I'm not the only woman who has struggled with the question of when enough preparation is enough. Similar feelings showed up in the stories of many of the women I interviewed. A woman's relationship with feeling ready for a career shift manifests in different ways. For some, it shows up as self-doubt. For others, it shows up as a maniacal motivation to succeed. For others, never feeling ready becomes a mask to cover up true career interests and dreams, sometimes for decades.

One story that stood out is that of Cary Lin, whom we meet in Chapter 5. Cary is an Asian American business leader and today is the cofounder and CEO of Common Heir, a bold, plastic-free skincare company that is revolutionizing sustainability within the beauty industry. Before becoming a cofounder and CEO, Cary had a career in consumer brand management. Cary was also my classmate in business school. When I caught up with her, she had recently moved to work on Common Heir full-time. I was excited to chat about her recent pivot. When we started our conversation, I asked Cary about the recent months that led to her pivot. But she told me we had to go back way further to understand her decision to pivot. Because in Cary's mind, her pivot had started a decade earlier, all the way back in 2011, when she first left her corporate finance job to explore the beauty industry. I was struck by this comment. *Wow*, I thought. *Ten years of preparation.* That level of discipline and planning struck me.

Cary's story begins when she graduated from college shortly after the 2008 financial crisis. The crisis got Cary curious about financial markets, and for her first job she joined a consulting firm that worked with financial institution clients. After a few years at the firm, Cary realized, *I don't find this interesting at all.* She followed her gut and left consulting for a role at an emerging luxury skincare brand, now a household brand, TATCHA. It was a glorified internship. She moved back home, earned minimum wage, and jumped around from digital marketing and product operations to finance. But Cary was hooked. Before her internship ended, she asked the founder—one of the first female Asian American entrepreneurs thriving in the beauty industry—for advice. "How do I become like you?" Cary remembers asking. Her boss told her about the path she had taken: start with an MBA and consumer brand work at a big-name company like Procter & Gamble.

That is precisely what Cary did. And that's where her pivot took root: the start of a decade of preparation for her final pivot to start her own company. Cary followed the path diligently. She earned her MBA, landed a competitive internship at Procter & Gamble, and after graduation started working at the Honest Company, where she led brand management for beauty and skincare products. After some time at the Honest Company, Cary wanted more experience at an early-stage company to further prepare for her transition to founder. She joined a company with a viral, overnight-success product to cure hangovers. She grew the company from $1 million to $10 million in revenue. She was gaining great experience, but at a cost: she was working around the clock. When she took her first vacation, she spent the week managing a PR crisis. After the vacation, Cary's husband asked her a blunt question: "When do you think you are going to feel like you've learned enough to do your own thing?"

The question opened Cary's eyes. What more was she waiting for? Cary remembered a book from business school. The book introduced the concept of founder fitness. Founder fitness was measured through a balance sheet of assets and liabilities. It was a pragmatic assessment of how ready someone was to become an entrepreneur. It asked practical, concrete questions: How much do you have in savings? Do you have kids? What level of experience do you have? Cary realized that her founder fitness would never be stronger. She had savings, a dual-income family, no kids, health insurance through her husband—the list went on. "I realized there was never going to be a better time," Cary told me.

She also had the experience, as Cary's husband reminded her. While she *still* felt she had gaps in experience, she also acknowledged that those gaps wouldn't be filled by joining another start-up that wasn't her own. There were some skills she would only learn after she took the leap and stepped into the cofounder role. "Sometimes you just have to bite the bullet and take the risk. If I had delayed and taken one more job before feeling ready to start my own company, it would have been a total waste of time. There was nothing I could have done to prepare me for the remaining skills I wanted." Cary likens entrepreneurship to a game of Monopoly. Except in this version of Monopoly, no one explains the rules to you. You learn by getting started and playing the game. When you pass GO for the first time, you realize you get to collect two hundred dollars. When another person buys a hotel, you realize hotels are an option. Trying to close that final gap to founder readiness while not actually being a founder was impossible. As Cary said, "I needed to learn the rest of the rules on my own."

Cary made the leap. In early 2020 she left her previous job and started her company full-time. Cary had spent over a decade preparing for this move. From her first internship in the beauty world, to business school, to experience in fast-growing start-up companies, Cary had checked virtually every box. She was ready.

THE CASE FOR BEING INTENTIONAL

Was Cary *too* ready? To become a founder, do you need a decade of carefully laid preparation? When I asked, "Do you wish you had jumped sooner?" Cary was torn. In some ways, yes, of course, she wishes she had started sooner. But Cary also understands that she was intentional and diligent for a reason. She knew how her identity as an Asian American woman affected her chances of success as a founder. She needed investment and support from within a male-driven business world. And that wouldn't come easy for her.

"I think women are intentional because we're punished for not being intentional," described Cary. "Unless you have access to your own capital, you have to use intention as a way to succeed. The bar is higher for women, so that's why intention becomes what so many women focus on." Cary understood that as a female cofounder, she would be under the microscope. Investors, whether consciously or subconsciously, would look for any reason to not take her business seriously. "In the back of my head, I wanted to stand in front of an investor and be able to say that my background is ideal for the vision of Common Heir. I wanted to feel confident and totally unassailable. If an investor was going to pass on me, I wanted to trust that it wouldn't be because of my background or my qualifications."

The experience for men is different. And Cary's inclination to check every box and form a bulletproof resume is informed by the realities of what it's like to raise venture capital (VC) for a start-up as a female founder. In 2018 female founders raised just 2.3 percent of VC funding, despite owning 38 percent of businesses in the United States.[1] The problem is worse for women of color, who have raised less than 1 percent of

Preparing to Leap

all VC funding since 2009.[2] The investment ecosystem itself is unbalanced. Less than 15 percent of VC investors are women, and 7 percent of VC investors are women of color.[3] Within the community, investors don't recognize the problem. Most investors believe women- and minority-owned businesses receive about the right amount of capital, with one in five even saying they receive more than they deserve.[4]

When Cary says the bar for women is higher, she is right. Any female founder sees this in anecdotal stories—such as the male founder with limited experience who walks into a pitch wearing a hoodie and walks out with millions in funding. Unfortunately, the data backs up these anecdotes. Investors view pitches differently depending on one's gender. An *identical pitch* switched from a male voice and image to a female voice and image receives lower ratings. The *identical pitch* with a male voice and image performs better.[5] Investors are more critical of women founders. Male founders are typically asked promotion questions, the questions that highlight the upside and potential gains of the investment. Female founders are asked preventive questions, those that highlight potential losses and risk. No surprise that entrepreneurs who are asked promotion questions (typically men) raise six times the capital compared to founders who are asked preventive questions (typically women).[6]

This type of gender bias also exists outside the VC world. Women face more criticism and barriers when pursuing career opportunities. For example, identical resumes perform better when the candidate's name is the male name *John* rather than the female name *Jennifer*.[7] Everywhere we look, data and experience show that candidates—whether pursuing VC funding or a new job—are not evaluated solely on their merits. Despite having the same exact pitch deck, female founders face tougher criticism. Despite having the same exact resume, female job seekers have a lower chance of getting the offer. Women implicitly know this reality. Our instinct to prepare, prepare, prepare is not irrational; it is highly rational and strategic.

STRIKING THE BALANCE

Women need to find the right balance when it comes to preparation and readiness. There is a reason that a woman's gut instinct is often to prepare, prepare, prepare. And that reason is not a *woman's problem*. It's a problem with the business environment in which women must operate. Women's ability to diligently craft and follow a plan is an asset that can help navigate the racial and gender biases that exist in our business worlds and our society. As you see with Cary, we are masters of strategically navigating those biases through diligent preparation, care, and motivation. If you are someone who feels, *I'm not ready*, use that as your superpower to craft a plan to get ready.

But at some point, you need to jump. You cannot—and should not—wait until you no longer hold any fears or worry about a career change. The truth is, you will never be fully ready. And you can't put your career dreams on hold to wait for gender and racial biases to go away. What you need to do is pair your pragmatic, strategic mindset with another mindset—a confident, empowered mindset.

Another female founder, Kim Malek of ice cream company Salt & Straw, talks about the power of women assuming the confidence that men have. "You have men in the world who wake up in the morning and think they have a good idea, and they can't wait to shout from the rooftops . . . [what] women tend to do—and what I did—is perfect things secretly for too long, which puts us at a disadvantage."[8]

Plan like you are a woman. But jump and act like you are not held back by your gender identity. With every career jump you make, you will demonstrate that you have more agency and empowerment over your career destiny. By taking your career into your own hands—by changing industries, starting over, or becoming the owner of a business—you experience empowerment. You show the control and autonomy you have over your career. You become the leader of your career destiny. This is a powerful expression that counteracts some (not all) of the limitations and biases that exist in the broad business world in which we must operate.

Preparing to Leap

Through the reflection questions below, start to give voice to the preparation you have already done—perhaps you are more ready than you think.

> **REFLECTION EXERCISE**
>
> 1. Do you believe you have 60 percent or more of the skills you need for your future career?
> 2. By waiting until you're 100 percent ready, what opportunities are you saying no to?
> 3. Who has the right to tell you when you are ready for the next step in your career?

CHAPTER 12

READY, SET, GO

START SAYING YES TO YOUR CAREER

Women spend a lot of time diligently preparing for career changes. They start by developing confidence in their abilities—or at least trying their darndest to!—and gathering a support team of people and resources who can help them on their journey. With the right mindset and support system, they can begin to execute. I always recommend executing with a test-and-learn approach, which is the focus of Chapter 10. This approach allows women to iterate and test their assumptions about the right career path to pursue. Through this strategy, women reduce risk and gain freedom to explore a wide array of career paths, since they have permission to be wrong and to change again. After testing and learning, when they are ready to commit to their pivot, women then work diligently to ensure they have the right skills, positioning, and story to bridge their experience to their future goals. Women put in a *lot* of strategy and work when they have a career goal in mind.

All this preparation is valuable and often necessary for you to make a big change in your career. But there is another truth: you will never feel fully ready. When you make a career change or pivot, you will never know everything that lies ahead. If you are waiting until you have full visibility, then you'll never make the jump.

Women must get comfortable being at a crossroads and simply deciding—seeing a fork in the road and choosing left or right. This can be unnatural if you are used to checking all the boxes and following the rules, expecting to be rewarded. We need more women to take their career into their own hands. Don't expect rewards. Go get those rewards. And the fastest way to take control and get rewards is to stop saying "No, I'm not ready" and start saying "Yes, I'll find a way."

BUT . . . ANALYSIS PARALYSIS

I am a Type A personality who loves checklists. I love having a plan. But detailed planning can be paralyzing. In consulting we talk about "paralysis by analysis"—analyzing and dissecting every piece of data with so much scrutiny that we never form an opinion or make a decision. We remain stuck, thinking, *How do I know what the right answer is?* In my own career, I fell prey to this. Anytime I considered a transition or new role, my instinct was to gather all the possible information. Networking calls with people in similar roles, interviews with employees, online reviews, an understanding of business performance, conversations with peers and mentors—the list goes on. When I decided to leave management consulting, I built an Excel spreadsheet with more than fifty data fields to assess every job opportunity: job salary, the job function, future career opportunities at the company, commute, manager style, work-life balance, and so on. Each field was an input pointing me toward the "right" path.

The goal of this spreadsheet was to help narrow down opportunities to identify the best fit for me. There was some value in the detail of the model. It helped me think critically about each new opportunity. But the desire to know it all also made the process terrifying and confusing. *What does my Excel model tell me? What does my gut tell me? Do I listen to myself or my Excel formula?* In the end, I had so many variables in my spreadsheet that every job computed to about the same score—a 7 out of 10. After months of input and thought and anxiety, my model told me, "Meh, they're all about the same." It was infuriating. And terrifying. I wanted to see the entire path. I wanted to calculate the risk. I wanted to find the *right answer*.

But our careers are not like a multiple-choice exam. There is no such thing as a right answer. Often our desire to get it right can keep us from going down the most rewarding paths. I was so afraid to pursue any career path with unknown elements that I ignored a lot of fantastic paths. Instead, I stuck to well-traveled routes that felt more comfortable because others had chosen that path too. But the right path for others is not a good way to define the right path for me. I wish I had thought about defining and climbing my *own* path. Instead, I avoided paths that, today, I can see could have been more fulfilling—and may have led me to more career potential and success too.

AT SOME POINT, WE MUST LEAP

Emily Golden had a successful, decades-long career in corporate HR working for well-known finance brands and overseeing all of HR, talent acquisition, and talent management. But throughout her career Emily had the persistent feeling that she hadn't arrived yet. She had a sense that there was something more out there. She would think, *One day I'm not going to do this anymore.* But when was "one day" going to be? Emily started to get sick of the narrative she told herself. A single New Year's Eve party set her on a new path. Emily described, "Everyone was making New Year's resolutions, and I was sick and tired of the same narrative and soundtrack in my head telling me that one day I'm not going to do this anymore. I finally felt that one day has to be now."

Emily reflected on the question of what she would do "one day," whenever that day came. She spent time reflecting on what brought her joy at work. She had a love for psychology and helping people, and she thrived in professional environments. Perhaps she would become a therapist. But while therapy was a fabulous tool to drive self-awareness, she wanted more action; she wanted to help individuals not only understand their behavior but also act on it. Then the light bulb clicked: coaching. "Coaching was a beautiful marriage of what I loved. I thought to myself, *Can you imagine waking up every day, and this is my job—people would pay me for this?* It fit me like a glove." But what did a road map to coaching look like? And how could she jump without knowing what the path would lead to?

Emily laid a foundation. She took on private coaching clients as a side hustle. She confirmed that she loved the work and could generate new clients. But then the time came for the big decision. Should she leave her corporate role and commit full-time? That jump had risk and required a leap of faith. Emily was scared. She did what she now coaches her clients on: she reminded herself that she would never know *exactly* what the road map looked like, but she could choose to trust herself and believe that she could navigate whatever the road threw at her. "When I'm working with clients, I tell them they need to trust what's outside of their control. When people are thinking about making a career pivot, they want to know exactly how to do it and what the road map is. But the reality is that, while you can set your intention, you have to move through life and allow the magic to happen."

It is good to prepare. It is good to have a plan. It is good to be disciplined and diligent about readying yourself for a change. But at some point, you must make the jump. As women, we need to get more comfortable *not knowing it all*. This requires acceptance of the fluidity of your forward career path. You may not know every twist and turn the path will take, but be okay with that. Do not expect to know everything. The truth is that you will never know it all, even if you stay on your current path. So let go of waiting to know it all. Just get started. If you never start, that "one day" moment will never come.

Ready, Set, Go

EVERY WOMAN IS UNCERTAIN: YOU ARE NOT ALONE

Saying yes and making the leap to move forward in your career—even if you don't feel ready or 100 percent confident—is crucial to your success. I know it does not always come easy. And that's true for nearly all women, including those who are highly successful.

Take Tina Fey. The one piece of advice she remembers jotting down during her improvisational acting classes was this: "Greet everything with Yes." That advice became ingrained in her. It led her to say yes to career opportunities even when she felt unprepared, uncertain, or not ready. As Tina describes, "I've felt maybe I'm not quite ready. Maybe it's a little early for this to happen to me. But the rules are so ingrained. 'Say yes, and you'll figure it out afterward' has helped me to be more adventurous. It has definitely helped me be less afraid."[1] That fearlessness led to many of Tina's biggest career breakthroughs: a job at *Saturday Night Live*. Moving up to be one of the head writers. Joining Jimmy Fallon for the "Weekend Update" segment of *SNL*. Each time she was terrified and petrified to say yes to these opportunities. But she still said yes.[2]

If we slow down and spend time perfecting our analysis—*Am I really ready for SNL?*—we forego opportunities, sometimes opportunities of a lifetime. Reshma Saujani, founder of Girls Who Code, talks about this in her book *Brave, Not Perfect: Fear Less, Fail More, and Live Bolder* and encourages all women to be brave like Tina.[3] Reshma believes that women's desire to be perfect and flawless holds them back. "I spent my entire life trying to credentialize myself, to be valedictorian, to get the 'perfect' big law job," says Reshma.[4] The problem? The desire to be perfect held Reshma back from her bigger potential. When she was focused on following the rules and coloring between the lines, she was also turning away from her larger career ambition: fighting for women and girls.

I love Reshma's story because it is also a story of failure. When Reshma first left her corporate job, it was to run for political office. The result? She lost. Many would define this as failure. But the broader result it had was a win for Reshma—she experienced the joy of going after something she wanted, regardless of the result. As she writes, "I took a risk; I failed miserably, but I felt more alive than I'd ever been because I was no longer filled with regret."[5]

Now Reshma urges women and girls to get more comfortable with failure. *Stop with the fifty-row Excel model*, I hear Reshma telling me. *Be brave, not perfect*. What Reshma teaches is that once women realize that mistakes won't kill them and that perfection is getting them nowhere, a new world of possibility opens. When we stop obsessing about making one wrong step in our career, we are suddenly less fearful of moving forward. We see that one misstep, or even two or three, is not the end of the world and not the end of a career.[6] The most legendary of women agree that failure should be accepted and even embraced if the other alternative is to never make a move. Oprah Winfrey emphasizes the importance of mistakes and failure, noting that mistakes are an opportunity to learn, teach, and push you toward being more of who you are.[7] And Arianna Huffington thinks of failure not as failure, but as *part of success*. We won't always make the right decisions—in fact we'll make plenty of big, bad decisions—but this is an inevitable part of the journey to success.[8]

MOVE TOWARD ACTION

Careful reflection is valuable as long as it does not keep you paralyzed. Women who are successful in making career changes are those who adopt rigorous preparation, but also have the confidence and fearlessness to jump before they have all the answers. This is especially critical for women who suffer from impostor syndrome or confidence gaps. If you wait until you have all the answers and feel fully ready, you will be waiting forever. You will never make the jump. But remember and be comforted by the fact that *you never truly know it all*, regardless of how much risk or how little risk you take. There will always be elements of your career that surprise you, ones that you are not prepared for. Why? Because it is impossible to know exactly how your future career path will unfold. It's important that we accept this as a universal reality, one that we cannot solve with more and more information or contemplation. The inability to completely plan for your career is unavoidable, whether you make a bold pivot or safely stay in your existing career lane!

To move toward action, we need to reclaim our relationship with mistakes. We need to give ourselves permission to be wrong. We need to think of mistakes not as failures, but as a part of our path to success. Accepting mistakes as part of our success is freeing. It takes pressure off the decisions we face. It helps us avoid analyzing the set of choices beyond what is helpful. It gives us the power to jump because we know that even if we miss the landing when we do, the jump is only one part of our story. We can make new decisions and choices that move us forward. When you are struggling with decisions, remember that there is no single "right way" to do your career. And when you do make the leap, regardless of the outcome, you will feel a stronger sense of engagement and satisfaction on your new career path. You will feel engaged. You will feel empowered. You will feel resilient.

To begin to reclaim your relationship with mistakes and failure, start by answering the following questions.

REFLECTION EXERCISE

1. What is important for you to achieve or prepare before you make a career change? Why?
2. When will you know when you are ready? How?
3. What will happen if you throw the "rules" out the window and just go for it?
4. If you had to live by the principle "brave, not perfect," how would your outlook on your career change?

PART III

THE WAYS YOU'LL WIN

CHAPTER 13

FEEL ENGAGED

Once women pivot to pursue a more authentic career trajectory, they are often surprised by how deeply engaged they become in their new work. After working in a role, or in an industry, or for an organization where they have felt friction or disillusionment, the level of engagement and interest experienced in their new work is refreshing. Women often report that they uncover a deeper pool of energy and motivation than they previously could access when following a career path that wasn't the right fit. They are engaged, sometimes for the very first time in their career. And for the 33 percent of women considering leaving or downshifting their career, this can feel like a revelation.[1]

UNLOCKING YOUR BEST ENERGY

I experienced this level of engagement when writing this book. When I first considered the prospect of writing a book, I wondered, *How will I stay engaged? How will I motivate myself?* I didn't have a boss telling me what to do. There were no calendar invites reminding me of deadlines, no salary hitting my bank account. In short, for the first time in my career, all my work would have to be self-driven and self-motivated. That was a scary thought.

It was scary because I hadn't experienced that level of self-reliance in my earlier jobs. By nature, I am a driven and motivated person. But in my work experiences, I was primarily motivated by external factors. I was anxious to impress a boss. I was competitive and wanted to be the best at my job. I wanted to keep earning my salary and receive my maximum bonus. These external validations were the primary sources of motivation. But I was largely in roles or industries where I wasn't *genuinely* interested in the task at hand. I did it for the external rewards and validation. But would I have signed up to do that work for fun? Absolutely not. So, faced with this new reality—writing a book *just to write a book*—I questioned whether I would succeed. How would I drag myself out of bed for the many hours required to conduct interviews, do the research, and write the manuscript? The idea of signing up to do something—just because—was strangely foreign. I didn't think I would have enough drive or motivation to get the job done. I was afraid to let go of the factors I had relied on in the past—external validation, prestige, and immediate financial rewards.

But what I discovered was refreshing. And it made me proud of myself in a way I had never experienced before. I got to test myself. Would I actually spend time interviewing dozens of women about their careers? Would I actually scour secondary research to understand what the data and academics who had committed their whole professions to these topics had to say? Draft chapters, rewrite them, and then rewrite them again? And the answer was a resounding yes. Although there was no salary hitting my bank account and no boss patting me on the shoulder, there was something new: I genuinely loved the work. Of all the motivating forces, I learned that this was the strongest motivation to keep a woman moving on her path. I was engaged. And the rest fell into place.

"CAN'T SLEEP" ENERGY

I am not the only woman who has felt a new level of engagement click into place after a career change. Many of the women I interviewed experienced a similar phenomenon. I'll tell you the story of Allison Whalen. Allison's story stands out to me because she unlocked new motivation at the time when you would *least* expect it—while she was a new mom, taking care of her first child, and returning to a full-time job at a fast-paced start-up that was growing exponentially. That's a time of life when everyone would understand if you were decidedly *disengaged*. But once Allison tapped into work that she found truly meaningful, she was motivated to work even harder.

Before Allison became a mom, she was working at a fast-growing start-up company called Managed by Q. It was a platform for companies to manage their offices. It was the first start-up she had ever worked for, and Allison was surprised how much she was enjoying her work. She learned that she was good at taking smart risks. She became the go-to leader to launch new lines of business. She launched the company in new cities and led the sales and operations teams. The job clicked. After her early career, where she worked in finance jobs that she never liked but kept for the paycheck and security of following a path, Allison found a role she really enjoyed. "For the first time in my career, I thought, *I'm really loving this. And I'm good at it*," remembers Allison. But then an exciting new life change—her pregnancy—took her on an unexpected detour where she discovered an even higher level of engagement and motivation.

Allison's pregnancy became the transformative moment of her career. During her pregnancy, she began planning for her maternity leave. She needed a plan for who would manage her team while she was out, how she wanted to be informed (or not) of major updates, and how other leaders could support her team while she was out. But she quickly realized that there was no plan for her to follow. When it came to pregnancy and maternity leave, especially in a start-up, she realized that there was no blueprint to follow. "It was such a shocking experience to me to have a child and go through maternity leave without any role model or any playbook. I didn't have any guide on how to take three months off of work, particularly in a really high-stress, fast-moving environment where I had direct reports." Allison felt the weight of the problem personally, but she also recognized the scale of this problem for *every* woman in the workforce. She knew she wasn't alone; she knew this must be a challenge for every working mother and parent.

Supporting parents during their parental leave was a big opportunity, and Allison became obsessed. She dug into the problems further. She stayed up late to read more and worked on the weekends to prototype a first solution. She put in this effort on top of parenting her first child. Over the course of six to nine months, together with a cofounder, she built the solution: Parentaly, a collection of online resources, community groups, and coaching designed to help women prepare for their maternity leave and thrive upon their return. When she launched her pilot program, she sent an email to friends and family asking for participants. She hoped to scrape together ten women to participate. Within a few days, nearly fifty women had signed up.

Allison's energy skyrocketed because she was working on a problem that she was personally invested in, one that she knew affected all working women, and one that she knew there was demand for. For almost a year, Allison worked on Parentaly as a side hustle. More late nights, more weekends, more effort squeezed in between her day job as a start-up leader and her other critical job as a parent. Then Allison's start-up was acquired, and she decided that this was an opportunity to focus on Parentaly full-time. She left the start-up and planned to take time off to enjoy some vacation weeks and spend time with her daughter and family. But instead, Allison found she was immediately drawn back into the Parentaly work. "I started on the business the next day," she recalls.

For the first time in her career, Allison was calling the shots on her own. She could take a sabbatical, sleep in, move slow. But also, for the first time in her career, she had never been so invested in her work. "It's because I was so obsessed with this problem that we know is a massive

Feel Engaged

problem. No one is working on it. There are lactation consultants and nannies, but no one is helping women navigate this extremely important time in their life of returning to work." Today Allison continues to build Parentaly. She is passionate about the huge problem Parentaly is solving. She is as engaged as ever—launching new programs with free resources for expecting mothers and a corporate offering for employers. And she is doing this all on her own terms, based on her own motivation, and now as a mom of three kids.

Allison's story reminded me of Katia Beauchamp, the founder of Birchbox. If you don't know Birchbox, it's a beauty subscription service with millions of active customers. Katia and Allison's stories follow a similar path—pivoting your career because you are *so* invested and motivated by the business problem you are solving. For Katia, her Birchbox story has its roots at business school. As a graduate student, Katia paired up with a classmate to write a business plan. They saw it as an academic activity—the only goal was to get experience writing the business plan itself, nothing more. But as Katia and her student colleague, future cofounder Hayley Barna, would soon realize, they uncovered a business plan they couldn't let go of.

Their plan was for a company in the beauty sector, and they fell in love with it. "When we saw this amazing opportunity waiting in beauty, we just couldn't settle. We couldn't sleep. We were so excited because we saw that in 2010, less than 3% of beauty was purchased on the internet, and it was the only category that wasn't changing its trajectory."[2] After graduating from business school, Katia and Hayley went on to build Birchbox, the beauty industry's largest subscription service. They've transformed the beauty industry and defined what it means to be a beauty e-commerce company of the future.

"Can't sleep" energy drives an intense level of engagement and motivation. Tapping into that energy makes work more enjoyable and rewarding. This is especially true for women, who often feel the opposite—a sense of *not* belonging at work or *not* doing purposeful work. When you're doing "can't sleep" work, you think about the reward in terms of happiness. You feel happier at work because you're doing what you love. But there is another important by-product of aligning work to your inherent interests or values, and it's this: doing so actually makes you *better at your job*. When you are engaged in your work instead of clocking in and out of a dreaded work environment, you are more likely to operate at your peak performance level.

START WITH YOUR STORY

For many of the women I interviewed, finding their "can't sleep" energy started with their own story. That is to say that the topics we are most passionate about are often the topics that define our own personal journeys. I think of Ellen Rice Chever, who pivoted her career to work in diversity, equity, and inclusion roles. Ellen's passion for DEI started with her own story and her experience as a young kid growing up in a White area and then her experience as a woman of color moving through a workforce where women and people of color were always underrepresented. This experience was a core part of her identity—the part of life that made her who she is. So why wouldn't this part of her identity also inform her career? As Ellen describes, "I spent my early childhood growing up in Minnesota in a predominantly White area. I was always 'the only.' And that continued throughout my life in different situations. Being the only woman or person of color in a room always made me curious. *Why am I the only? Surely there might be others that want and should be here too?* I've been asking that question since I was a child. At some point I also got curious about how to solve it. That's what led me to think about a career in diversity and inclusion."

Ellen's life experience didn't just point her toward DEI work—it also made her more successful at that work. Ellen is an expert by training, but she is also an expert by living. Her personal story makes her more committed and more prepared to do her job. Today, this approach of aligning one's personal story with one's career is the top career strategy she offers to others: "Aligning your career with your purpose is the *best* thing to do for your career. It's highly strategic. It will let you endure longer and go further in your career. I tell people you need to match your purpose with your skill sets and also what's unique about you. Your lived experience gives you so much perspective and outlook. For example, I can study DEI&A in a book, but my lived experiences also uniquely qualify me to do the work because I understand it in a very personal way. You can't learn that in school. It's your very own lived experience, and it's competitive because nobody else has it."

Leslie Forde, the founder of the market research company Mom's Hierarchy of Needs, shared a similar story of aligning her career with her personal experience. In Leslie's case, the defining experience was her transition back to work after having her second child. After receiving a promotion at eight months pregnant, she finished her parental leave and returned to work with an expanded team and bigger responsibilities. Adjusting to a bigger job at work and double the kids at home was daunting. As Leslie remembered, "I was in the wee hours of the night trying to shield my baby's co-sleeper with a pillow so the glow of my computer wouldn't wake her up. And I was exhausted. I was working all the time. There were so many days where I didn't even remember driving to the office. And when I had my space to think, I realized, *Wow, I don't feel like I'm doing this well. Am I the only one who feels this way?*"

Around this time, one of Leslie's clients needed research on moms and stress. Leslie quipped that moms and stress had to do with the existence of a "mom's hierarchy of needs." And something clicked inside. She became obsessed with the idea of this hierarchy of needs—because she was living it. Leslie mapped out what a mom's pyramid of needs looks like, the specific levels of needs, and how frequently moms are meeting them. She turned the hierarchy into a formal presentation. She created a survey to get insights from hundreds of women experiencing motherhood. And from there, the business was set in motion. Leslie's lived experience as a mom not meeting her hierarchy of needs is what gave her unique interest in this topic. And it sustained her, because she intimately knew the value of solving the problems that prevent mothers from meeting their needs. Leslie's lived experience fueled her commitment to her business and her ability to execute it.

THE BENEFITS OF FLOW

The deep engagement women get from aligning their career to that "can't sleep" track or to your personal lived experience is similar to the concept of *flow*. Flow was first introduced in 1990 in the book *Flow: The Psychology of Optimal Experience* by psychologist Mihaly Csikszentmihalyi. Since then, Mihaly's 2014 TED Talk has more than five million views and has popularized the concept. The original book argues that happiness levels can be shifted by introducing flow—a state in which people are their most creative, productive, and happy. Mihaly found the impacts of flow to be true across a diverse range of people and professions and across classes, genders, ages, and cultures. The word *flow* came from his interview subjects, with an unusual amount describing their optimal performance state as instances when work simply "flowed out of them" without much conscious effort. From there, the concept of flow was born. Mihaly describes *flow* as "a state in which people are so involved in an activity that nothing else seems to matter; the experience is so enjoyable that people will continue to do it even at great cost, for the sheer sake of doing it."[3]

Flow also sounds a lot like my experience writing this book. Feverishly typing at my keyboard, unaware if I'm even blinking, and waking up an hour later with a drafted chapter. Or listening to a woman's story only to glance at my phone and realize we've gone past our time limit by an hour. It sounds like Allison's story too—staying up late to work on Parentaly, all while taking care of a newborn and getting back into the swing of her full-time role after her own parental leave. The exhaustion of new parenthood and a return to work would surely qualify as "at great cost," as Mihaly writes, but Allison still chose to do the work. Flow also sounds like the experience of Katia and Hayley becoming obsessed with their business plan. Their flow was so strong they felt they had no alternative but to continue moving ahead.

Since Mihaly, more research has shown more benefits of flow. As Mihaly proposed, working in a state of flow makes us happier. We enjoy what we are doing more. Neurochemists have studied the chemical released in the human brain during a state of flow. A cocktail of endorphins, along with norepinephrine, dopamine, anandamide, and serotonin—all pleasure-inducing, performance-enhancing neurochemicals that improve everything from muscle reaction times to pattern recognition to lateral thinking—are released during flow.[4] So working in a state of flow doesn't just affect your level of enjoyment and happiness (though to be clear, it does). Working in a state of flow also *makes you better at what you do*. In a flow state you are more likely to reach your peak performance. Advancements in brain imaging technologies show what happens to the human brain when we're in a state of flow. And what happens is best described like this: the brain's extrinsic system, or the *conscious* processing function, is swapped out for the intrinsic system, also known as the *subconscious* processing function. Why does that matter? Well, the extrinsic system in our brain is slower and requires more energy. On the other hand, the intrinsic subconscious system is a lot faster, and it's more efficient. "It's an efficiency exchange," describes neuroscientist Arne Dietrich.[5]

Another fascinating finding is that flow affects how we self-monitor. You might not know the scientific definition of self-monitoring, but I guarantee you have felt the effects of it: "Self-monitoring is the voice of doubt, that defeatist nag, our inner critic," writes Steven Kotler in a *Time* article that delves into the science of peak human performance.[6] Another amazing benefit is that during a state of flow, we deactivate the part of our brain responsible for much of our self-monitoring, inner critic behavior. I am going to pause and repeat this: *when we work in a state of flow, we let go of our inner critic*. If you are a woman in corporate America, you know the power of this statement; you have experienced the devastating effects of impostor syndrome, confidence gaps, lack of belonging, or outright bias and sexism experienced in the workforce. Releasing your inner critic is transformative. Or, as Steven explains, "The result is liberation. We act without hesitation. Creativity becomes more free-flowing, risk-taking becomes less frightening, and the combination lets us flow at a far faster clip."[7]

THE POWER OF A PIVOT

All the benefits of flow—happiness, performance optimization, and the release of your inner critic—are so valuable for women. Being happier, better, freer, and more confident at work is what so many women are *craving* in their careers. Women so often worry that a career change is a selfish or indulgent act. *Shouldn't the job I have now be good enough?* But understanding the value of flow equips women with a powerful bit of knowledge: pivoting to a career where you are engaged is not just an indulgent act; it is a strategic act. Pivoting to an engaged career will lead to more opportunities for flow. More opportunities for flow mean you will be optimizing your performance and becoming *better at work*. When we think about it in this way, career changes stop being the thing that will set you back in your career. They start being the thing that will move you forward! Pursuing a career that is engaging will allow you to tap into your highest performance and your highest career potential.

I want more women to believe in their right to pursue a career where they are engaged. Not just because you deserve to be happy and satisfied at work (though you do), but also because pursuing a career of purpose in which you feel engaged and motivated is one of the most strategic things you can do for your career. Fighting for a career that is engaging is not self-indulgent. It's not just about searching for happiness. It's about good career strategy. By finding and pursuing the *right career for you*, you will perform at your best. And that path is what's most likely to take you the furthest.

I encourage you to explore the concept of flow in the context of your own career. When do you experience flow in your current job?

Feel Engaged

Outside your job? If you could do anything, what would you do? These questions can feel lofty or pie in the sky. But allow yourself to dream and think in silly ways. Whatever you say, reflect, or write is not a commitment. Was your dream as a kid to become a pop music star? Write it down. Like most women, this is not the precise dream you will follow. But writing it down might allow you to understand something else about your work—that you crave creativity, love making others feel good, or value being recognized for your work. Doing this reflection should make you more comfortable identifying those areas of flow where you are happiest and performing at your best. Start by answering the questions below. They are pointing you in the right direction.

REFLECTION EXERCISE

1. When have you experienced flow in your career and how did it make you feel?
2. If you were fully engaged and invested in your work, how would it affect your performance?
3. What is an opportunity in your career that you "just want" or "just need" to do, even if it seems a little out there?

CHAPTER 14

BE EMPOWERED

When women pursue a career change or pivot, they learn what it feels like to be empowered. They experience what it is like to take back control of their career. They no longer listen to the voices around them suggesting that they pursue a traditional, safe path, even when it's not *right for them*. Instead, when women make a change, they learn to control their own career destiny. An important mindset shift follows. Women start to understand that there is no one way to do their career. They move from looking for success by always following the rules and checking the boxes to understanding that, in the game of their career, they are the only ones who can write the rules of winning. The importance of that transformation should not be understated. It is a *massive shift* in how women view their careers and their ability to pursue what they want out of them.

WHEN YOU'RE NOT IN THE DRIVER'S SEAT

In my career, I rarely felt like I was in the driver's seat. The career decisions I made were typically made in an autopilot mode. I was letting my career happen *to me* instead of making my career happen. At times it was even worse. I wasn't even on autopilot; I was in the back seat of the car. I sought out the opinions of everyone around me, while the one opinion I trusted least was my own. "Is this a good move? What do you think? What would you do?" My head and my heart could scream at me to turn left. But if even one or two voices told me to turn right, I would silence myself. I was not in control of my career. My career was controlling me.

Driving in autopilot or pressing the cruise control mode is tempting, especially for women. Making smart, strategic career decisions is hard. It requires hard work and thought. It bubbles up difficult emotions like fear, uncertainty, and anxiety. Hard decisions are hard. This is especially true for the many women who suffer from impostor syndrome. When you work in a biased, unequal corporate environment where you are told, either explicitly or implicitly, that you are less than—well, you may start to believe it. And you begin to doubt the value of what you offer in the workforce. But you also begin to doubt your decision-making power. It's easy to convince yourself that *they know better*.

Navigating your career from cruise control is also fueled by confidence gaps. When women feel that they are behind or less than their peers, then they immediately operate from a place of catch-up. You stop focusing on the long-term destination you want to reach. Instead, you start to focus on the few cars that are in front of you. Your goal is no longer to reach your destination. Instead, your goal becomes catching up with those cars. But what if those cars aren't going in the right direction? When you're in autopilot mode, you're not likely to notice, and it doesn't matter anyway. Your only goal is to get rid of the horrible feeling that you are not going fast enough to keep up. You want to prove that you are fast enough or good enough or smart enough. And you'll do whatever it takes to get there.

Fear and impostor syndrome drove so many of my biggest career decisions. When I look back at major career choices—like attending business school or starting a career in management consulting—I can now see that I was not proactively owning my career decisions. Instead, I went to business school because I thought *I must*. I looked at people around me in business roles, and I felt so insecure and inferior. As I zoomed in more and more on that fear, I entered autopilot mode. *This is what I need to do to keep up with the cars ahead of me*. It was the same experience when I started consulting. But this time, the sacrifice was greater. I accepted my consulting role with pride, but also with terror. The thought of weekly travel and working up to eighty hours made me sick. My head and my heart kept shouting: *This is not for you. This is not for you. Can't you see?* But I couldn't see. I couldn't resist the powerful pull of cruise control.

It's important to distinguish that being in the driver's seat has very little to do with achieving success. By traditional standards, I had a lot of success. I worked for great companies, with competitive income and access to powerful communities of people. But success, privilege, or achievement did not equate to empowerment over my career. This is a juxtaposition that many women shared with me in their interviews. Many women who pivot are highly successful in their original careers. They acknowledge and are grateful for the opportunities they have earned. But at the same time, that privilege and achievement did not lead to feeling empowered. No matter what level of success, so many women still felt disempowered. They became passive players in their own career journey. They clung to an established career path, and they didn't feel they could jump off the track. Or they clung to the ideals of a "good career" that society had ingrained in them, and they couldn't define success on their own terms.

TAKING CHARGE

Career pivots are a way to reclaim empowerment over your career. Taking the risk of a big career change is often the moment in which women—sometimes for the very first time in their lives—start to put their careers in their own hands. After five, ten, twenty, or more years, women finally take charge and become the CEO of their own career.

Take Tamara Warren. Tamara built a successful career as a journalist, writer, and editor. When she moved back to her home city of Detroit, she focused her writing and journalism on the automotive industry. Cars are a critical part of the local economy and daily life in Detroit, where major manufacturers like Ford and GM have their headquarters. Tamara was one of the few female reporters in the country who covered the automotive beat, and that motivated her. She wanted to make a name for herself as a great automotive reporter—and as a great *female* automotive reporter. Early in her career, Tamara thrived as an individual reporter, but as Tamara got further into her career, she wanted to lead teams and take on leadership roles. But with that new ambition, Tamara realized that her growth seemed stunted.

Tamara had the right experience, but she struggled to get elevated to leadership roles within the publishing organizations where she worked. Tamara didn't expect to simply be handed big opportunities that she didn't deserve. The problem was that she knew she deserved them, but she was never offered them. "So many times in my career, I saw that I worked harder, had more experience, had a following—all the things. And yet I would consistently get offered the number-two job and never the leadership role," Tamara described. She watched her peers—all of them men—make progress while she was passed up for opportunities.

The male-dominated world of cars produced a form of sexism that was subtle. Tamara doesn't believe male leaders were *actively* discriminating against her as a woman, but they weren't embracing her either. As Tamara remembers, "I came to realize over the years that editors and business leaders wanted to see themselves in others. When someone came up the ranks who reminded leaders of themselves, that was a huge benefit, and that person shot up high and shot up fast. The problem for me is that I knew that no male leader was going to see himself in me." The sexism that Tamara experienced was subtle enough to go undetected by the men who were inflicting it (but never feeling the pain). But that pain was potent enough to be felt and understood by Tamara. Tamara wanted to be a leader and advance in her journalism career. But she saw how her future career would play out staying in an environment where, to get ahead, you had to look like those around you. The result? She would never have a chance to win. She could tread water, sure, but she would not advance. The path became clear: to stay meant to lose.

Tamara felt it was time to take the reins back and reclaim control of her career potential. To get in the driver's seat, she had to shift her career elsewhere. Tamara was scared to pivot her career and make a change. But when her fears popped up, she reasoned with herself that at least she would have a *chance* at success. "If I leave now, at least I'm in charge of transforming my own reality instead of handing it over to someone else and being in a position where I don't feel empowered at all," Tamara told me. So she planned her next move. She launched her own venture, Le Car, an online platform inviting women into the automotive experience through car matching, concierge services, and car content curated for women. Today, life as an entrepreneur is no less challenging or time consuming than life as a journalist. But this time Tamara is in the driver's seat. And she wouldn't have it any other way.

Tamara is not alone. Other women I interviewed described the powerful impact a career pivot had on their sense of control over their career. Taking a risk and making the decision to go after something new or different—something *they* wanted—is an experience in empowerment. Susan Aminoff departed from her long-term plan to climb the ladder in marketing, stepping off her track to explore other business functions like strategy and operations. Making the decision to step off the track was revelatory for Susan, showing her that she had power over her career identity and permission to evolve and change. "I learned that I'm in charge of my own tapestry. And the threads can be made up of whatever I want. If I decide I want red instead of green—nobody's going to tell me that it shouldn't be red. Green might work for you, but it's not going to work for me. And I'm not going to apologize for that," said Susan.

Carrie Collins is an ex-lawyer turned higher education administrator. When I asked Carrie what gave her the confidence to make a big pivot out of a prestigious track (law), she talked about empowerment. She said she always understood that she was in control of her career destiny—that she was the architect of her own career.

ESCAPING THE GLASS CEILING

Tamara's story of workplace inequity holding her back is not unusual. Women's desire to be fully in control of their career is often the result of painful inequities. Women realize they have to proactively control their career because they can't trust anyone else to get them where they want to go. In these cases, making a career pivot becomes a strategy not only to pursue the work that they want but also to escape the glass ceiling that limits them. When women like Tamara feel like they are getting passed up for opportunities, it's because they are.

Let's look at promotions. Women and men *want* to be promoted in about equal numbers. However, women are 15 percent less likely than their male peers to receive that promotion. If all women participate in this system, it will take us at least one hundred years to achieve gender parity in the C-suite.[1] But maybe men are doing something different or something better than women to deserve these promotions? No. In fact, if anything, women are doing more and performing better than men. Study after study shows this. In one, researchers used performance reviews and actual sensors to track women's and men's activity at work: the number of face-to-face meetings they participated in, productivity rates and how much they got done during the day, and performance on evaluations. The performance was consistent across men and women.[2] Research proves what women instinctively know: this is not a problem with *the woman*; this is a problem with *the system*.

Challenges for women of color are significantly more profound.

Women of color have equal and often *higher* ambition when it comes to career advancement. For example, almost *two-thirds* of Black women in the United States say they want to make it to the top of their profession—that's about twice the number of White women aiming for the same goal,[3] and it's also higher than White male counterparts.[4] Women of color also lead in terms of their desire to be promoted.[5] But the ability to achieve these goals looks different for Black women and other women of color. For example, Black women receive less support from managers. They are less likely to interact with senior leaders. They are much less likely to be promoted to the manager level. And from there, representation declines even more—Black women hold less than 2 percent of VP and C-suite roles. While all women face the challenges of navigating gender bias, women of color are burdened with the additional and arguably bigger hurdle of navigating racial bias. Half of Black women worry that their race will limit their opportunity to get ahead in the workforce.[6]

For many women, a career pivot is a strategy to reclaim control over their potential. Women are leaving toxic corporate environments where their success is limited. Instead, they are looking for equitable companies that will authentically value, support, and elevate them. This is a powerful shift. Women are learning that they should not contort themselves into a corporate system that will never fit them. Instead, they are yearning for the opportunity to bring their full selves to work—and assurance that the corporate system will support them. A career change is a way to demand this. By shifting to a new organization, industry, or job where you will have greater opportunity for career advancement, you are taking back power over your career—the power to value yourself, your worth, and your career potential more than the security or stability of the existing corporate system you're in, no matter how scary it might feel to change.

BE YOUR OWN BOSS?

Increasingly women are leaving the companies that don't serve them—and not just turning to *another* company but turning to themselves to create their own company. This is not a new trend; it is not a post-pandemic shift. More women were starting their own businesses well before the pandemic emerged. Between 2014 and 2019, the number of women-owned businesses grew over 20 percent—compared to just 9 percent overall growth.[7]

Empowerment is a key motivation behind women's decisions to pursue entrepreneurship, solopreneurship, or small business ownership. Women want to feel empowered; they literally want *to have the power* over their career and work experience. When you are the CEO of your company, you don't face a glass ceiling—at least not within your own organization.

I heard this message loud and clear from the female business owners I interviewed. Women pursued entrepreneurship or small business ownership as a strategic move to reclaim control of their career fate. Women were sick of dealing with toxic work environments, passed-up opportunities, and unequal pay. They were sick of fighting the system. This was the mindset for Mari-Anne Chikerema Chiromo, who launched her first entrepreneurial endeavors after becoming a mom. Mari-Anne was working in Big 4 consulting and big tech while learning how to be a new parent, but despite all that—perhaps *because* of all that—she felt compelled to add entrepreneurship to her plate. After having her son as a single parent, she had what she describes as a catalytic moment of thinking. "I want to be able to be in control of my destiny. Do I have the energy to be a good mum *and* keep fighting for a seat at the proverbial table? Why aren't I diverting my energy into building my own table . . . and chairs . . . including one for my son?" Women—especially mothers, and even more so single mothers—are determined to achieve career and financial success. But they would rather bet on themselves than a corporate system that has repeatedly shown very little progress toward real equity. As Mari-Anne described, entrepreneurship was a bet on herself rather than a blind faith in the system—a system that many women don't feel they can rely on to deliver opportunities to themselves or their children anytime soon.

Mari-Anne mentioned anecdotally that she had read somewhere the greatest number of entrepreneurs was among ethnic minorities, especially women. She's correct. Almost one in five Black women are running or in the process of starting their own business. That is a rate higher than White women and White men.[8] Unfortunately the corporate reality for women of color is that they have more to endure and less to gain. It can be "easier" for women of color to walk away from corporate roles because they know it is so much harder for them to exist, thrive, and advance in that environment. The tax that women of color pay is never-ending. There is always more labor to be done—work harder, tread lighter, speak less, but be more. Mari-Anne was not surprised by the statistic that minority women were choosing entrepreneurship. *Not* choosing to pursue your own venture is even more exhausting. The extra work that women of color must do in the workforce creates exhaustion, as Mari-Anne described. "Doing your job—and to a high level just to bust perceptions, but also doing this whole evangelizing, this convincing, this treading so carefully because you can't make mistakes, and navigating landmines you don't even fully understand." The list of additional labor described by Mari-Anne and others is endless. At some point—what's the point?

OWN IT

Whether you choose a career change *within* a corporate environment or a career pivot *out of* a corporate environment, your change is powerful. You are overcoming uncertainty, fear, and guilt. You are reclaiming ownership and agency over your career destiny. When you make a proactive career shift decision, you are *owning your career*. Instead of your career happening to you, you are making your career happen. You are in the driver's seat. And you get to decide where to go next. A successful career pivot does not mean the next phase of your career will be without setbacks or ups and downs. Those are inevitable. But career pivoting sets you up to build a unique type of career resilience—a resilience that prepares you for the twists and turns that will come, regardless of which path you take.

Reflect on the questions below to determine whether you are acting like the CEO when it comes to your career.

> **REFLECTION EXERCISE**
>
> 1. Who controls your career trajectory today?
> 2. When have you pressed cruise control during your career and how did it affect your career path?
> 3. What steps can you take to have more power over your career trajectory?

CHAPTER 15

BUILD RESILIENCE

Women benefit from many positive impacts of a career change. They feel a greater sense of power over their career and their life, and they show up more engaged in their work. But perhaps the greatest benefit of a career change is more subtle; it is simply that women learn how to take a risk. Once women make one career change, they realize how resilient they are to make future changes. Women learn that pivoting or reinventing their path is not only doable; it often launches them on a *bigger* and *better* career path filled with more potential, more fulfillment, and even more traditional success.

For many women, including career changers, the act of pivoting is not always a choice. Many times, it is a necessity. From layoffs to the demands of caring for children or aging parents, women are often faced with challenging circumstances that *force* them to reinvent. Faced with many pressures and not enough flexibility, women must roll up their sleeves and get creative to *find another way*. Even if you do always have the gift of choice and options, career changes are still likely to be a reality you face. Today, careers are fluid. Gone are the days of sticking with one company for multiple decades of your career. The new normal is change.

So what's the best way to prepare to thrive in a modern career economy where pivoting is the new normal? The best way is to get comfortable with change—to accept and expect that change will be a part of your career story. And the most effective way to familiarize yourself with change is to try it out. This was true for so many of the women I interviewed. Their pivots often led them to more fulfillment and longer-term success. But often that success was not the biggest win that came from their career pivot. Instead, the biggest win was the act of learning how to pivot. Experiencing the art of a career change was the greatest reward of all. Women realized that they are capable of change—not just for their specific, most recent pivot but at any point and at any time during their career or their life. Through the act of reinventing their career, women learn resiliency—the ability to adapt, react, and move forward—and these are the skills that are needed most to thrive in today's modern career economy, where the new normal is ongoing career change and evolution.

LEARN FROM THE JOURNEY

It's the journey, not the destination. Nearly every woman I interviewed for the book agreed with this statement. They benefited as much from the *journey* of career change as they did from the change itself. The destination is important. Women are uprooting their career paths and changing for a reason, after all. But the journey has an even deeper, longer-lasting impact. For example, when a woman successfully leaves her corporate job to start her own company, she proves to herself that she can be an entrepreneur. But really she is proving to herself something much bigger. She is proving to herself that *she can be anything*. She knows how to reinvent herself. And now that she's an entrepreneur, she knows she could do it all again. This is why women see so much value in the *resiliency* that a career change teaches them. If you give a woman a new job, you fulfill her for a period. If you teach a woman the art of how to reinvent her career trajectory, you fulfill her for a lifetime.

I heard this loud and clear in so many women's stories. Tamara Warren, the automotive reporter who left the world of journalism to start her own company, was terrified to start over and become a business founder, but she still did it. And when she did, she accessed a newfound courage and resilience. She realized that there is never the perfect tool kit of skills for any job and that she had more of a foundation than she gave herself credit for. The same methodologies and skills that Tamara used in journalism stuck with her through her pivot, and it turns out they were helpful in the business world too. But more than that, Tamara experienced the transformation of battling through her fears and still finding success.

Tamara told me the story of being accepted into the start-up accelerator Tech Stars. She felt intimidated and out of her league. She told me she was surrounded by ten other computer scientist founders; implicit in that story was her feeling that she might not have as much to offer as these scientists. But within two weeks of the program, she was leading workshops for all the founders on how to tell your start-up story in a compelling way. It was an epiphany moment for Tamara. There would always be moments when she felt inexperienced or lacked confidence. But she learned that those moments, too, would pass. And she had proven her resiliency to battle through those moments and make it.

Other women talked in depth about the important lessons their career pivot taught them when it comes to resiliency. Susan Aminoff had planned her marketing career and path to chief marketing officer since she was sixteen years old. She realized mid-career that she wanted to broaden her career and step off her well-planned path, but that decision came with bumps along the way. She lost out on dream jobs and promotions that, at the time, crushed her pride and confidence. When she reentered the job market in 2001 after September 11, she met resistance. And yet Susan sees these setbacks as some of the most valuable experiences of her career. She ended up believing in herself and her capabilities more *because of* these "failures." Each time she went through a setback, she moved forward and found a solution. And each time, she gained more confidence and resiliency. "I started to have some agility and resiliency. I started realizing, *This doesn't mean my life is over. It just means I need to pivot.*" Every time Susan navigated a change, she was learning that these were just turns in the road. She would continue to forge ahead on her career path—and perhaps discover a better path. For Susan, this shift was dramatic—a tectonic-level shift in how she valued herself and what she is capable of.

THE VALUE OF RESILIENCY

Today's career economy virtually *requires* that we become resilient to career change. Change is just a reality of the modern working world. Across generations, polls show that as many as 90 percent of workers are either not engaged or actively disengaged from their jobs—often a precursor to a career leap.[1] Why is it that the modern career path looks like this?

To better understand why career change is our new normal, I spoke with Gayle Grader, the director of executive career development at the MIT Sloan School of Management. For decades Gayle has watched careers unfold for the hundreds of MIT Sloan business school students with whom she works each year. Gayle acknowledges the fluid nature of careers today. She believes that the prevalence of career changing is a result, in part, of the optionality that growing technology provides to job seekers every year. "Decade by decade, technology has enabled a lot more optionality. New technology systems, then eventually job boards, allowed people to become more aware and made it easier to remove some of the barriers. And it led to this fluid nature that we now need to approach careers over a lifetime." We pursue change in our careers because we can see more options.

Gayle is right. And there's more, too. When I realized how important resiliency—the ability to adapt to adversity or change—is for the modern career path, I started to research careers and resiliency. I came across HBR research on the emergence of a career-resilient workforce. I was shocked when I looked at the publication date: 1994. The article talked about exactly what I saw with the career changers I interviewed, almost thirty years later. More and more, the workforce was requiring that people be resilient to changes and evolution throughout their careers. Change was the new normal. Employees needed to be highly adaptable to adjust to a rapidly changing work world that required rapidly changing skills. This dynamic was changing our relationship with employers, too—a sea change in attitudes and values that changed our loyalty and our usual view of a career path. For earlier generations, a career meant staying at one company and specializing in a certain area. "These days, both companies and employees are healthier if employees have multiple skills, if they can move easily across functional boundaries, if they are comfortable switching back and forth . . . and feel comfortable moving on when the right fit within one company can no longer be found."[2]

A career-resilient workforce is like the test-and-learn approach that I talk about in Chapter 10. A test-and-learn approach encourages women to view career planning and management as an iterative process with rounds of action, reflection, and change throughout their careers. This iterative process means that you can continually define new goals and new possibilities. It increases satisfaction and fulfillment because you maintain the ability to continually explore your career. You leave behind a fixed mindset and instead are constantly learning and progressing. And with every hypothesis that you test, you *get better at managing your career*. Just like little babies have leaps of learning, you also have leaps of learning and aha moments the more that you explore and learn. You gain more knowledge about yourself, your career, and how you can achieve the most success and fulfillment.[3] With every hypothesis you test, you become better at building and testing new hypotheses—and ultimately planning and managing your career over the long term.

When you become resilient and open to change throughout your career, it also emboldens you to go after new opportunities. Change becomes less scary. I remember my interview with Lizzie Jones, who moved from a recruiting career to launch her own coaching company to then pivot back into the tech world as a marketer. When Lizzie took her coaching business full-time, I asked if she was hesitant to leave behind the stability of a corporate role. Hesitation is common as women often see this type of career change as a landmark, one-time, career-defining move. But Lizzie didn't see the change in exactly this way. As Lizzie described, "Careers are so fluid that I knew I would probably switch again. That really unstuck me. I didn't think about it like, *If I make this move, that's it. I'm signing my life away.* It's hard to make a commitment like that. Instead, I saw that my decision to go full-time didn't mean that I was going to do it forever. I could go back to corporate if I wanted to." Lizzie's modern outlook on the nature of career changing and resiliency helped give her confidence and comfort to make the jump.

HOW TO START: START WITH CHANGE

Change requires resiliency. So how can you build it? The good news is that resiliency—specifically, career resiliency—is a quality you can develop. However, it requires that you take the jump. Gayle Grader sees hundreds of career changers each year—at MIT Sloan, 85 percent of MBA students are considering a career change—and she agrees that building resilience is a great predictor of success. But the best way to build resiliency is to *get experience doing it*. Those who tend to struggle most with career changes are those who don't have any experience doing it. "I can tell immediately," Gayle told me, "those who are going to find it easier are those who made diverse choices in their existing career path. The people who struggle the most are those that have ten or fifteen years of experience with very few transitions; they've stayed on the same career path the entire way."

There are a few reasons why these types of candidates struggle with the level of change that is so common in today's careers. The chief

Build Resilience

difficulty is simple: they don't have experience with change when it comes to their career. But less obvious is how these types of people seek out career opportunities. In a nutshell, they don't. For individuals who have constantly been on the same career path, they are used to opportunities *coming to them*. They are less likely to be proactive and go out into the market to *look for* the right opportunities. They are most comfortable in a standard career path, where they are told what comes next; figuring out what's next on their own feels paralyzing. Gayle shared the story of one student who came to the career development office: "I have a military leader with twenty-five years of experience in the military. His whole career path was dictated by the military. He expected that the career development office would tell him the answers. But we're not doing that."

Kate Bennett, the MBA admissions director at Harvard Business School and former talent manager at a top global consulting firm, also sees new career changers every year in her work. The number-one factor that she says predicts individuals' likelihood in succeeding at a career change? It's the same: whether they have experienced taking risks and making changes in their careers. Kate shares that the outcome of the change—whether they failed or succeeded when they made the change—doesn't matter. In fact, trying something and failing can make people better equipped to reinvent. As Kate shared, "It's actually *helpful* when people have experience with something not working. It's harder to take a risk if every step you've taken has been planned and you've never failed at anything. It makes that risk seem harder. Whereas if you have experiences that show you can be not great at something and still get back on the path or get on another path, it makes it easier to take risks." The longer you wait to take any risk in your career, the more difficult it becomes when you want, or are forced, to make a change. The experience of taking risks and pivoting your career helps people to build up confidence and resilience. "The more experience with change and taking that risk you have, the easier it becomes," says Kate.

Research agrees that resilience is a skill we can learn. Dr. Kristen Lee is a behavioral scientist who studies resilience. Her research shows that building resilience is like strengthening a muscle—the more you practice, the stronger you get. The more you fail and get back up, the more resilient and fearless you will become. As Kristen explains, "My work has shown me that deliberate, intentional effort to cultivate resilience can bolster our inclinations for it. When we think of it that way, we can understand that there are specific habits, behaviors, and mindsets that help us foster it."[4]

THE CASE FOR CHANGE

Resiliency is a skill that you need to succeed at work today. Changes across industries, the economy, and technology are taking place at a lightning pace. The result is that our working world favors a career-resilient workforce and a test-and-learn approach. You need to be able to adapt and change over the course of your career. There's no choice to opt out. And this is not just a one-time occurrence, either. Career changes will repeat themselves throughout the duration of your career. It is not about a single pivot. It is about preparing yourself for ongoing, long-term career evolution where you make many pivots at many points. And resiliency is *especially* important for female career changers who face additional adversity in executing their careers. Confidence gaps, lower appetite for risk-taking, the impostor syndrome, and lack of women in leadership positions can make it scarier for women to consider a career change. And, once committed to a switch, women still face sexism, racism, and gender bias in evaluation, hiring, promotions, and funding.

The good news is that resiliency can be learned, practiced, and built up like a muscle. And the best way to do that is to get comfortable with change. To start taking risks. To make that pivot. I hope that you see pieces of yourself in the stories shared in this book. I believe that it is through stories that we find the most motivation. And there is no better way to start building your resilience than getting motivated to go after that career pivot, switch, or change—sooner rather than later.

Using the questions below, start reflecting on what would be possible through a career pivot. If you were to make a change, what new career story would you write?

> **REFLECTION EXERCISE**
>
> 1. Some say careers are a ladder. I say careers are a river. How would you describe your career?
> 2. What would you prove to yourself simply by making a career pivot?
> 3. How will change be a part of your career long-term? What would be the cost of avoiding change?

CONCLUSION

WE NEED TO TALK

We are in an unprecedented time of complexity when it comes to navigating our careers. Careers used to be like ladders—predictable, linear, singular. But today, careers are more like rivers, with twists and turns, influenced by the environment around you, and moving in directions that you can't always predict.[1] The pace of technology is moving faster than ever. New companies are forming, and entirely new *industries* are emerging, which means that you literally do not know what opportunities will present themselves in five, ten, or twenty years. While careers are becoming more complicated, we continue to double down on having a career as a fundamental part of our identity.

The complexity of careers is especially true for women. That complexity has been exacerbated over the last three years since the global pandemic broke out. Women rising to leadership ranks in the workforce today are the first generation of women who grew up being told they could have it all. But women feel gaslighted because—as their hopes, dreams, and ambitions mounted—what the world failed to tell them is that "having it all" actually means "doing it all." Undersupported and overwhelmed, women are crumbling. Women continue to be underrepresented in leadership positions. They continue to operate in male-dominated environments that were never built for them, where they are often isolated as the only woman at the table. They face bias in hiring, promotions, work assignments, venture capital funding, mommy penalties—the list goes on. Women of color operate at the intersection of sexism and racism, which offers more devastating setbacks, frustrations, and challenges. But throughout it all, women are told to soldier on. To carry the feminism flag that the generations before them did. To be grateful for the opportunities that their mothers, and their mothers, and their mothers never had.

Enough is enough. It's time to think differently. It's time to rewrite the rules. It's time to take back control of our careers. To define success *on our own terms*, rather than on the false narratives we've been fed growing up and rising in the workforce. If success means working within sexist corporate structures that limit our potential, taking on second and third labor shifts at home, and doing it all with a smile, then it's time to blow up that version of success.

When I interviewed women who were doing it differently—leaving corporate roles, taking leaps, starting their own businesses—I was inspired by their ability to say no. To reject the traditional paths laid out in front of them, and instead fight for something different: a career path, perhaps nontraditional, but one that felt right to them. As the pandemic has raged on since 2020, we have heard and seen more stories of women leaving the workforce, women scaling back, and women recalibrating. Not always because they wanted to—but because they needed to. And perhaps the global pandemic is the explosion women have been waiting for—the moment when enough truly is enough. When we burn it all down, and out of the ashes, we rise.

It is time.

EMBRACE YOUR CAREER AS AN EMOTIONAL JOURNEY

Women are told to think about careers "rationally"—as pragmatic decisions, often based on dollars and cents or black-and-white factors. And

Conclusion

when I first started my research interviewing women for this book, I had my rational analyst hat on. I expected to uncover the pragmatic know-how for doing your career "right": the tangible tips and tricks for pivoting, a framework, a road map, or concrete steps. But very quickly I saw that this was a different assignment. As women shared their career stories, what flowed out was not a clear-cut set of instructions on how to pivot. Instead, what flowed was their emotions and the deeply personal journey that had accompanied their career and life decisions. We are told to approach our careers like analysts. But when it comes to the real world, we don't make career decisions like robots. We make career decisions like *people*, and that means from a place of deep emotion.

So, when you reflect on your career right now, if you're thinking, *Why do I feel so dissatisfied? So alone? So guilty? So reluctant and afraid to do anything about it? Why am I feeling all these emotions?*, I'm here to tell you that you are not alone. All of us experience these emotions when it comes to our careers. When women feel these emotions, many of us tend to think something is "wrong," and we focus on how to quickly fix and eliminate our feelings. We pathologize these emotions, just like we do with impostor syndrome. But when we realize that almost every woman feels this way—as I had the chance to see through my interviews—we finally understand a fundamental truth. We are not broken because we have worries, fears, frustrations, or regrets when it comes to our careers. These emotions are not the end of our career dreams. They do not signal that we're not cut out for a competitive career. Emotions are simply human experiences. And we build and experience our careers as humans.

But we can harness these emotions more effectively when we build a tool kit of mindsets, support systems, and strategies to navigate our careers. When we look for role models who inspire us and plant the seed of possibility for the future. When we adopt a positive mindset to not only consider failure but also consider wild success. When we remember that taking risks is a necessary part of any good career strategy. When we build the right team of supporters who lift us up and allow us to invest time and resources in our career. And when we remember that we can test and learn and build detailed preparation strategies, but ultimately acknowledge that we must make the leap at some point.

When you use this tool kit to actively build your career, that is where the magic happens. You feel more engaged. You experience flow. You operate at your peak performance. You pursue work that is authentic to you. You feel more empowered and develop more confidence, ownership, and command over your career.

IT'S YOUR TURN

This book shares the real-life stories of dozens of women—and represents the stories of hundreds of more women who are not featured by name—who are navigating their career journeys and fighting for a more authentic and meaningful career. They are women who have taken a chance. Women who have struggled. Women who are figuring it out. Women who are thriving. Women who lost. Women who won. Every story is different. There are stories from women late in their careers and early in their careers. There are stories from moms, single moms, and nonparents. There are stories from primary breadwinners, lifestyle business owners, and stay-at-home moms. The stories are from everywhere, but the beauty in each of these stories is that *every story belongs to each individual woman.* These are not the narratives we heard growing up: have it all; opt out; lean in. These are the *real* stories that women wrote for themselves. These women were brave enough to let it all go or blow it all up—to take the leap and reinvent the career of their *own* dreams.

The final question is: What story will you write for yourself?

APPENDIX

REFLECTION TOOL KIT

PART I: WHY YOU FEEL THIS WAY

Chapter 1: DISSATISFIED

Women feel dissatisfied in their careers for many reasons. But even when we know "this isn't it," it's hard to take action. We convince ourselves that aligning our career with our inherent interests is a luxury or unrealistic. Or we stress about the challenges and risks that come with change. When you're feeling stagnant or like there is something more out there for you, don't get bogged down by the distress of feeling unhappy. Instead, think about those feelings as signals that you're ready for new opportunities—some of which may be bigger, better, and lead you to more success long-term.

Ask yourself:

1. What brings me the most energy at work?
2. How could I do more of that work?

3. How would my life change if I felt more satisfied with my career?
4. How does my feeling of dissatisfaction affect my career success?
5. What pains do I feel today? What am I dissatisfied with? What work do I dislike doing?

Chapter 2: ISOLATED

Women are underrepresented in leadership, business, tech, government, and nearly all positions of power. When you are the only woman at the table, it is natural to feel lonely, misunderstood, or like you don't belong. It is also common to feel psychologically unsafe or to be exposed to aggressions that wear you down. Belonging matters. And it affects your ability to succeed at work. Keep track of the people and work environments that break you out of feeling isolated and come up with a game plan to seek out more of those people and communities. Your success depends on it.

1. In what moments do I feel most isolated at work?
2. What type of people inspire me the most when it comes to my career?
3. How does my work environment (the people, the culture, the mission) influence my level of career success?

Chapter 3: GUILTY

This generation of women building our careers has been told that we can have it all. We are reminded of the increased opportunities we have relative to generations of women before us. When we struggle to succeed in a system that was never designed for us, we are told to lean in more. All of this supports the narrative that you do not deserve your own fulfillment in your career—that good enough should be, well, good enough. There's a sense that you have an obligation to serve others' expectations for your career rather than your own. There's also a sense of being stuck—the feeling that you do not have the right to critically evaluate your career path. Simply put, you need to move beyond this guilt. You need to remember something as a matter of fact: you have the right to build your own career.

1. Who has a right to be a decision maker when it comes to my career?
2. How will a career change allow me to contribute or create impact in my community?
3. What truths would become clear if I were to focus only on myself?

Chapter 4: RELUCTANT

The financial implications of a career change can create reluctance and a hesitation to pursue your authentic career goals. Financial security is powerful—financial freedom is nearly priceless. Your career decisions should be rooted in the reality of your financial security. But sometimes women use financial security as a scapegoat and justification to stay in their comfort zone. If you are feeling reluctant, analyze what is fact and what is narrative. Are there reasonable facts that support you staying in place where you are? Or is this a narrative you are telling yourself based on facts that are no longer true or never were?

1. How will you know when you have achieved financial security? Will it make you less hesitant when it comes to your career?
2. When you are reluctant to consider a change, what opportunities are you saying no to?

3. If you could devote your career to anything and still have the money and lifestyle you needed, what would you be doing with your career?

Chapter 5: AFRAID

Making any meaningful change in your career is a scary prospect. There is the fear of failure, judgment from others, or making a misstep. When you work in an environment that holds women to higher standards, reinforces confidence gaps, and doesn't support women in overcoming impostor syndrome, there is real reason to feel unsure. But fear is a universal emotion. And in fact, fear can lead you to great places. Distinguish between good fear that is pushing you to challenge yourself and bad fear that is simply holding you back.

1. What are you most afraid of when it comes to your career?
2. Which failure has helped you most in your career?
3. I know you spend time thinking about what would happen if your career shift wildly failed. But what might happen if your career shift wildly succeeds?

PART II: HOW TO EMBRACE . . .

Chapter 6: ROLE MODELS

Inspiration for your career comes from all places. Sometimes, it's from role models—functional role models who have gone down the same career path you want to travel or inspirational role models who embody a mindset toward their career growth that you want to emulate. Look for role models everywhere you go. Let them inspire you, accept their help, and study their blueprints. But remember, they are only models, and your path will be unique to you.

1. No filter: What did you love to do as a kid? What did you want to be when you grew up? Why?
2. Whose career do you admire most? Why?
3. What element do you most want to add to your career identity?

Chapter 7: NEW POSSIBILITIES

Women are often raised to be box checkers. We are told we will find comfort if we stay within the lines. It can feel easier to follow the narrow narratives that society presents to us—lean in, opt out—instead of writing our own unique stories. There is always opportunity to forge a different path outside of the few well-established ones. But it takes courage to open your eyes and acknowledge those possibilities. The number-one thing I hear from women is "I don't know what I want to do," but in all cases, women know a lot about what they want. The greater challenge is giving ourselves permission to unlock that truth and go after it.

1. What unexpected event has most positively affected your career?
2. Up until now, what rules have governed your career? What's one rule you want to get rid of? What rule will you replace it with?
3. What are five career opportunities you would immediately say yes to if they presented themselves?

Chapter 8: RISKS

When we think of career changes, we tend to focus on what we will give up. We worry about the risks and bad potential outcomes. The truth is that there is risk anytime you make a change. But there is also possible reward. Risk is a strategy to propel your career forward faster and further. You need to balance your focus on potential risks with equal attention to potential rewards. As many times as you mutter to yourself, "What if this fails and blows up in my face?" you should be muttering the same number of times, "But what if this wildly succeeds?" This shift pushes you to think bigger and plant more ambitious goals and visions.

1. What career risk has paid off most in your career?
2. How will not taking risks negatively affect your career?
3. What safety nets and support systems do you have (or can you build) to reduce your risk?

Chapter 9: YOUR SUPPORTERS

Women are expected to provide support. But when it comes to building successful and fulfilling careers, we need to receive support too. The right support system will help you see your full potential, help you build confidence and conviction even within work environments that are not designed with your success in mind, and help you feel the risk is not solely on your shoulders. Yet building these support systems is not easy; the status quo will not give you the level of support you need—nowhere close. You need to proactively design an operating model at home that enables you to give your career the time and dedication it requires. And you need to actively develop a professional network to support you in the workplace.

Reflection Tool Kit

1. What is a moment in your career when you've thought, *I'm great at what I do?*
2. Who are your biggest career cheerleaders? What do they say are your strengths?
3. How would more confidence change the way you navigate your career?
4. What daily habit could you introduce to drive more free time at home?

Chapter 10: THE TEST-AND-LEARN APPROACH

When we think of career pivots, we often envision a bold, spontaneous decision—quitting the job on a Friday and enrolling in culinary school on Monday. But most career pivots happen methodically over a long period of time, with months or years of contemplation and execution. This is a good thing. You don't have to be a spontaneous risk taker to reinvent your career. And you don't have to know exactly what you want to do either. Instead, you can adopt a test-and-learn approach. You can experiment with hypotheses and small changes that help you refine your understanding of what you want. And you can do this again and again throughout your career. This is the reality of the modern career path. Gone are the days of a fixed ladder that you climb. Today's career path meanders, with ongoing shifts and redirections.

1. What's one thing you can do this month to start moving your career in a new direction?
2. What are three elements you want to incorporate into your future career?

3. Earlier in your career, what assumptions or hypotheses did you have about work that proved to be wrong?
4. How will moving in incremental steps help your career development?

Chapter 11: PREPARING TO LEAP

Women tend to diligently prepare for their career change. You might be inclined to prepare until you have checked every box. This instinct is based in an unfortunate reality. The rules of the game are different for women. Managers consistently underestimate women's potential, venture capital funds consistently reject or more harshly evaluate female founders and founders of color—the list goes on. You might prepare until you are bulletproof, in part because that's what you must do to win. But if you are always preparing, you will never get going. Women need to find the right balance of preparation. We need to prepare with an understanding of the "rules," however unfair. But then we must leap as though we are not held back by any gender identity.

1. Do you believe you have 60 percent or more of the skills you need for your future career?
2. By waiting until you're 100 percent ready, what opportunities are you saying no to?
3. Who has the right to tell you when you are ready for the next step in your career?

Chapter 12: READY, SET, GO

Once you're ready and set, you must go. Most women never feel fully ready to go. But at some point, you have to say yes, and you have to jump. If you rely on an "I will do it one day" mindset, I can promise you:

one day will never come. The ability to move forward in your career even when you don't feel 100 percent ready or confident is critical to your success. Reframing your relationship with failure is a powerful first step. Instead of cringing at the prospect of failure, bake failure into your plan. You will fail at points. You will make bad decisions. Failure is part of a successful career.

1. What is important for you to achieve or prepare before you make a career change? Why?
2. When will you know when you are ready? How?
3. What will happen if you throw the "rules" out the window and just go for it?
4. If you had to live by the principle "brave, not perfect," how would your outlook on your career change?

PART III: THE WAYS YOU'LL WIN

Chapter 13: FEEL ENGAGED

When women pursue their authentic career goals, they become deeply engaged. When you align your career with an authentic view of who you are, you unlock your best energy. You start to flow. You click into a new gear. You perform at your best. Women experience more happiness and freedom. But there is more than just enjoying their work. *Women who pivot to pursue authentic career goals are also better at their jobs.* They are operating at their fullest potential and able to execute and achieve more. Pursuing an authentic career is not just fluffy—it is a strategic decision that sets you up for long-term career success and endurance.

1. When have you experienced flow in your career and how did it make you feel?

LEAP

2. If you were fully engaged and invested in your work, how would it affect your performance?

3. What is an opportunity in your career that you "just want" or "just need" to do, even if it seems a little out there?

Chapter 14: BE EMPOWERED

It is easy to operate your career on autopilot—to press the cruise control button and follow an established path where you've seen others succeed. But only when you take charge and proactively establish your career goals do you become truly in charge of your career, act as the CEO of your own career, and determine your career trajectory. This is important for all women because we operate in environments that are not designed to propel us forward. The status quo autopilot mode doesn't serve us, so we *especially* need to get in the driver's seat. Career pivots are a way to do just that—to reclaim empowerment over your career and where you are headed.

1. Who controls your career trajectory today?

2. When have you pressed cruise control during your career and how did it affect your career path?

3. What steps can you take to have more power over your career trajectory?

Chapter 15: BUILD RESILIENCE

There are many benefits to a career change. But one of the greatest is the opportunity to learn the art of career changing in and of itself. Career changes are the new normal. Today's career economy *requires* that we become resilient to career change. And the people who are most prepared and resilient to change are those who have done it before. The

Reflection Tool Kit

actual change associated with a pivot or reinvention—moving industries, starting your own business, or leaving corporate—is important. But nearly all women agreed that the more profound impact is the recognition that if you've reinvented once, you can do it again. When you learn how to career change, you learn how to navigate a lifelong career.

1. Some say careers are a ladder. I say careers are a river. How would you describe your career?

2. What would you prove to yourself simply by making a career pivot?

3. How will change be a part of your career long-term? What would be the cost of avoiding change?

NOTES

Introduction

1. Michelle Obama, *Becoming* (New York: Crown, 2018).
2. Deloitte, "Why Women Are Leaving the Workforce after the Pandemic—and How to Win Them Back," *Forbes*, July 1, 2021, https://www.forbes.com/sites/deloitte/2021/07/01/why-women-are-leaving-the-workforce-after-the-pandemic-and-how-to-win-them-back.
3. Gallup, *State of the Global Workplace* (New York: Gallup Press, 2017), https://fundacionprolongar.org/wp-content/uploads/2019/07/State-of-the-Global-Workplace_Gallup-Report.pdf; Gallup, "How Millennials Want to Work and Live," 2016, https://www.gallup.com/workplace/238073/millennials-work-live.aspx.
4. Anne Marie Segal, "How Analysis Paralysis Can Kill Your Career," *Forbes*, February 14, 2018, https://www.forbes.com/sites/forbescoachescouncil/2018/02/14/how-analysis-paralysis-can-kill-your-career/.
5. Paul McCaffrey, "How to Hate Your Job Less," *Prevention*, July 18, 2012, https://www.prevention.com/life/a20432358/aligning-personal-interests-with-job-makes-for-happier-employees/.
6. Mike Oppland, "8 Ways to Create Flow According to Mihaly Csikszentimilhalyi," *Positive Psychology*, April 28, 2020, https://positivepsychology.com/mihaly-csikszentmihalyi-father-of-flow/.
7. Caroline Castrillon, "Why Resilience Can Make or Break Your Career," *Forbes*, October 13, 2019, https://www.forbes.com/sites/carolinecastrillon/2019/10/13/why-resilience-can-make-or-break-your-career.

8. Vanessa Boris, "What Makes Storytelling So Effective For Learning?" *Harvard Business Publishing Corporate Learning*, December 20, 2017, https://www.harvardbusiness.org/what-makes-storytelling-so-effective-for-learning/.

Chapter 1

1. Beth Castle, "Why So Many Women Want to Change Careers," *Fast Company*, September 6, 2019, https://www.fastcompany.com/90398601/why-so-many-women-want-to-change-careers.
2. Robin Hilmantel, "Ina Garten: I Don't Believe in Making Goals," *Time*, February 4, 2016, https://time.com/4198968/ina-garten-making-goals/.
3. Hilmantel, "Ina Garten."
4. Abigail Hess, "Stanford Researchers: 'Follow Your Passion' Advice Could Make You Less Successful," CNBC, June 22, 2018, https://www.cnbc.com/2018/06/22/stanford-researchers-following-your-passion-makes-you-less-successful.html.
5. Hess, "Stanford Researchers."
6. Hess, "Stanford Researchers."
7. Michal Bohanes, "'Following Your Passion' Is Dead—Here's What to Replace It With," *Forbes*, July 5, 2018, https://www.forbes.com/sites/michalbohanes/2018/07/05/following-your-passion-is-dead-heres-what-to-replace-it-with/.
8. Jenny Blake, *Pivot: The Only Move That Matters Is Your Next One* (New York: Portfolio/Penguin, 2016).
9. Blake, *Pivot*, 3.
10. Anna Mikulak, "Employee Interests Predict How They Will Perform on the Job," Association for Psychological Science, August 27, 2012, https://www.psychologicalscience.org/observer/employee-interests-predict-how-they-will-perform-on-the-job.
11. Anthony K. Tjan, Richard J. Harrington, and Tsun-yan Hsieh, *Heart, Smarts, Guts, and Luck* (Boston: Harvard Business School Publishing, 2012).

Chapter 2

1. Annamarie Mann, "Why We Need Best Friends at Work," *Gallup*, January 15, 2018, https://www.gallup.com/workplace/236213/why-need-best-friends-work.aspx. See also Evan W. Carr, Andrew Reece, Gabriella Rosen Kellerman, and Alexi Robichaux, "The Value of Belonging at Work," *Harvard Business Review*, December 16, 2019, https://hbr.org/2019/12/the-value-of-belonging-at-work.

Notes

2. "Women in America: Work and Life Well-Lived," *Gallup*, 2016, https://www.gallup.com/workplace/238070/women-america-work-life-lived-insights-business-leaders.aspx.

3. Mann, "Why We Need Best Friends."

4. Frances Dodds, "We All Need Work Wives: Here's How Bosses Can Encourage Female Friendship," *Entrepreneur*, February 26, 2020, https://www.entrepreneur.com/article/346799.

5. Catalyst, "Women in Male-Dominated Industries and Occupations," October 29, 2021, https://www.catalyst.org/research/women-in-male-dominated-industries-and-occupations/.

6. Sarah K. White, "Women in Tech Statistics: The Hard Truths of an Uphill Battle," *CIO*, January 23, 2020, https://www.cio.com/article/3516012/women-in-tech-statistics-the-hard-truths-of-an-uphill-battle.html.

7. National Center for Women and Information Technology, "Women in Tech: The Facts (2016 Update)," May 13, 2016, https://ncwit.org/resource/thefacts/.

8. Michaela Dempsey, "Silicon Valley Is Where Women Go to Fail—Unless They Do These Three Things," *Fast Company*, July 24, 2019, https://www.fastcompany.com/90380422/silicon-valley-is-where-women-go-to-fail-unless-they-do-these-three-things; David Bell and Dawn Belt, "Gender Diversity in Silicon Valley," Harvard Law School Forum on Corporate Governance, April 30, 2019, https://corpgov.law.harvard.edu/2019/04/30/gender-diversity-in-silicon-valley/.

9. D.I., "The Vile Experiences of Women in Tech," *The Economist*, May 3, 2019, https://www.economist.com/open-future/2019/05/03/the-vile-experiences-of-women-in-tech.

10. Tanya Tarr, "By the Numbers: What Pay Inequality Looks Like for Women in Tech," *Forbes*, April 4, 2018, https://www.forbes.com/sites/tanyatarr/2018/04/04/by-the-numbers-what-pay-inequality-looks-like-for-women-in-tech/.

11. Matthew Hughes, "Exclusive: Research Shows Many Women Developers Are Stuck in Junior-Level Roles," *Next Web*, March 1, 2018, https://thenextweb.com/news/exclusive-research-shows-many-women-developers-stuck-junior-level-roles; HackerRank, "2018 Women in Tech Report," 2018, https://research.hackerrank.com/women-in-tech/2018/.

12. Catalyst, "Women in Male-Dominated Industries and Occupations."

13. Mariela V. Campuzano, "Force and Inertia: A Systematic Review of Women's Leadership in Male-Dominated Organizational Cultures in the United States," *Human Resource Development Review* 18, no. 4 (2019): 437–469.

14. Dilshani Sarathchandra, Kristin Haltinner, Nicole Lichtenberg, and Hailee Tracy, "'It's Broader than Just My Work Here': Gender Variations in Accounts of Success among Engineers in U.S. Academia," *Social Sciences* 7, no. 3 (2018), https://doi.org/10.3390/socsci7030032.

15. Yue Qian and Wen Fan, "Men and Women at Work: Occupational Gender Composition and Affective Well-Being in the United States," *Journal of Happiness Studies* 20 (2019): 2077–2099.

16. Campuzano, "Force and Inertia."

17. Catalyst, "Sexual Harassment in the Workplace: How Companies Can Prepare, Prevent, Respond, and Transform Their Culture," March 15, 2018, https://www.catalyst.org/research/sexual-harassment-in-the-workplace-how-companies-can-prepare-prevent-respond-and-transform-their-culture/.

18. Sarathchandra et al., "'It's Broader than Just My Work Here.'"

19. Sarathchandra et al., "'It's Broader than Just My Work Here.'"

20. Sarathchandra et al., "'It's Broader than Just My Work Here.'"

21. Dempsey, "Silicon Valley."

Chapter 3

1. Sheryl Sandberg with Nell Scovell, *Lean In: Women, Work, and the Will to Lead* (New York: Knopf, 2013).

2. Deborah Spar, "Why Do Successful Women Feel So Guilty?" *The Atlantic*, June 28, 2012, https://www.theatlantic.com/business/archive/2012/06/why-do-successful-women-feel-so-guilty/259079/.

3. Ellen McCarthy, "She Famously Said That Women Can't Have It All: Now She Realizes That No One Can," *Washington Post*, August 26, 2016, https://www.washingtonpost.com/lifestyle/style/she-famously-said-that-women-cant-have-it-all-now-she-realizes-that-no-one-can/2016/08/26/889944e4-5bf3-11e6-831d-0324760ca856_story.html.

4. Anne-Marie Slaughter, "Why Women Still Can't Have It All," *The Atlantic*, July–August 2012, https://www.theatlantic.com/magazine/archive/2012/07/why-women-still-cant-have-it-all/309020/.

5. Slaughter, "Why Women Still Can't Have It All."

6. Slaughter, "Why Women Still Can't Have It All."

7. American Society of Plastic Surgeons, "Women Underrepresented in Plastic Surgery," October 2, 2017, https://www.plasticsurgery.org/news/press-releases/women-underrepresented-in-plastic-surgery.

Notes

8. Cherisse Berry, Dineo Khabele, Crystal Johnson-Mann, Ronda Henry-Tillman, Kathie-Ann Joseph, Patricia Turner, Carla Pugh, et al., "A Call to Action: Black/African American Women Surgeon Scientists, Where Are They?" *Annals of Surgery* 272, no. 1 (2020): 24–29.

Chapter 4

1. Michelle Obama, *Becoming* (New York: Crown, 2018), 89.

2. Obama, *Becoming*, 132.

3. Oprah Winfrey, "Michelle Obama Gets Candid with Oprah about Her New Memoir, *Becoming*," *Town and Country*, November 12, 2018, https://www.townandcountrymag.com/society/a25011108/oprah-michelle-obama-becoming-interview/.

4. Jenny Blake, "Pivot: The Only Move That Matters Is Your Next One," Talks at Google, October 26, 2016, https://www.youtube.com/watch?v=dL7LBoGIHZM.

5. Shana Lebowitz, "Graduates Who Flock to Wall Street, Silicon Valley, and Big Law in Search of Prestige Might Be in for a Harsh Wake-Up Call Only a Few Years Later," *Business Insider*, December 13, 2018, https://www.businessinsider.com/people-quit-high-paying-jobs-prestige-less-important-2018-12.

6. Lebowitz, "Graduates Who Flock to Wall Street."

7. Lebowitz, "Graduates Who Flock to Wall Street."

8. *Dictionary.com*, s.v. "prestige," accessed August 17, 2020, https://www.dictionary.com/browse/prestige.

9. Shana Lebowitz, "A Harvard Psychologist Says There's a Question to Ask Yourself When You're 'Successful' But Unfulfilled," *Business Insider*, January 13, 2017, https://www.businessinsider.com/harvard-psychologist-susan-david-identify-core-values-2017-1.

10. Shana Lebowitz, "The Question a Harvard Psychologist Says You Need to Ask Yourself If You're Feeling Unfulfilled," *World Economic Forum*, January 30, 2017, https://www.weforum.org/agenda/2017/01/successful-but-feel-unfulfilled-heres-what-a-harvard-psychologist-suggests.

11. J. David Creswell, William T. Welch, Shelley E. Taylor, David K. Sherman, Tara L. Gruenewald, and Traci Mann, "Affirmation of Personal Values Buffers Neuroendocrine and Psychological Stress Responses," *Psychological Science* 16, no. 11 (2005): 846–851.

12. J. M. Harackiewicz, E. A. Canning, Y. Tibbetts, C. J. Giffen, S. S. Blair, D. I. Rouse, and J. S. Hyde, "Closing the Social Class Achievement Gap for First-Generation Students in Undergraduate Biology," *Journal of Educational Psychology* 106, no. 2 (2014): 375–389.

13. Arghavan Salles, Claudia M. Mueller, and Geoffrey L. Cohen, "A Values Affirmation Intervention to Improve Female Residents' Surgical Performance," *Journal of Graduate Medical Education* 8, no. 3 (2016): 378–383.

14. Lebowitz, "The Question."

15. Chimamanda Ngozi Adichie, *We Should All Be Feminists* (New York: Anchor Books, 2014), 27.

16. Katie Abouzahr, Matt Krentz, Claire Tracey, and Miki Tsusaka, "Dispelling the Myths of the Gender 'Ambition Gap,'" Boston Consulting Group, April 5, 2017, https://www.bcg.com/publications/2017/people-organization-leadership-change-dispelling-the-myths-of-the-gender-ambition-gap.

Chapter 5

1. Andrew Leigh, "Are Women Financially Conservative or Just Economically Realistic?" *InvestmentNews*, May 12, 2014, https://www.investmentnews.com/are-women-financially-conservative-or-just-economically-realistic-2-56726.

2. Doug Sundheim, "Do Women Take as Many Risks as Men?" *Harvard Business Review*, February 27, 2013, https://hbr.org/2013/02/do-women-take-as-many-risks-as.

3. Elaine M. Lui and Sharon Xuejing Zuo, "Measuring the Impact of Interaction between Children of a Matrilineal and a Patriarchal Culture on Gender Differences in Risk Aversion," *PNAS* 116, no. 14 (2019), https://doi.org/10.1073/pnas.1808336116.

4. Liu and Zuo, "Measuring the Impact."

5. Pauline Rose Clance and Suzanne Ament Imes, "The Imposter Phenomenon in High Achieving Women: Dynamics and Therapeutic Intervention," *Psychotherapy* 15, no. 3 (1978): 241–247.

6. L. V. Anderson, "Feeling Like an Impostor Is Not a Syndrome," *Slate*, April 12, 2016, https://slate.com/business/2016/04/is-impostor-syndrome-real-and-does-it-affect-women-more-than-men.html.

7. Alison Wood Brooks, Laura Huang, Sarah Wood Kearney, and Fiona E. Murray, "Investors Prefer Entrepreneurial Ventures Pitched by Attractive Men," *PNAS* 111, no. 12 (2014), https://gap.hks.harvard.edu/investors-prefer-entrepreneurial-ventures-pitched-attractive-men.

Notes

8. Arielle Pardes, "In a Banner Year for VC, Women Still Struggle to Get Funding," *Wired*, October 11, 2021, https://www.wired.com/story/in-banner-year-for-vc-women-still-struggle-to-get-funding/.

9. Sheryl Sandberg, "Federal Government to Silicon Valley," *When to Jump* (podcast), October 23, 2017.

10. Ann Shoket, "Don't Call It a Pivot," *The Riveter*, accessed May 3, 2022, https://theriveter.co/voice/how-to-pivot-ann-shoket/.

11. *Fortune* Editors, "The Best Advice I Ever Got," *Fortune*, October 25, 2012, https://fortune.com/2012/10/25/the-best-advice-i-ever-got/.

12. Ginny Brzezinski, "Meredith Vieira's Life-Changing Advice for Women Who Want to Make a Career Comeback," MSNBC, February 5, 2020, https://www.msnbc.com/know-your-value/feature/meredith-vieira-s-life-changing-advice-women-who-want-make-ncna1130701.

13. *Dictionary.com*, s.v. "pivot," accessed November 23, 2022, https://www.dictionary.com/browse/pivot.

Chapter 6

1. Rockefeller Foundation, "Women in Leadership: Why It Matters," accessed May 3, 2022, https://www.rockefellerfoundation.org/wp-content/uploads/Women-in-Leadership-Why-It-Matters.pdf.

2. Thekla Morgenroth, Michelle K. Ryan, and Kim Peters, "The Motivational Theory of Role Modeling: How Role Models Influence Role Aspirants' Goals," *Review* of *General Psychology*, December 1, 2015, https://doi.org/10.1037/gpr0000059.

3. Oprah Winfrey, "Michelle Obama Gets Candid with Oprah about Her New Memoir, *Becoming*," *Town and Country*, November 12, 2018, https://www.townandcountrymag.com/society/a25011108/oprah-michelle-obama-becoming-interview/.

4. Ruth H. V. Sealy and Val Singh, "Role Models, Work Identity and Senior Women's Career Progression—Why Are Role Models Important?" *Academy of Management Annual Meeting Proceedings* 2006, no. 1 (2006), https://doi.org/10.5465/AMBPP.2006.22898277.

5. Wendy Murphy and Kathy Kram, *Strategic Relationships at Work: Creating Your Circle of Mentors, Sponsors, and Peers for Success in Business and Life* (New York: McGraw Hill, 2014), 7, 37.

6. Wendy Murphy, "How Women (and Men) Can Find Role Models When None Are Obvious," *Harvard Business Review*, June 1, 2016, https://hbr.org/2016/06/how-women-and-men-can-find-role-models-when-none-are-obvious.

Chapter 7

1. Courtney Connley, "How a Career Change at 32 Led Ava DuVernay to Become the First Black Woman to Direct a $100 Million Film," *Make It*, March 10, 2018, https://www.cnbc.com/2018/03/09/a-career-change-at-32-led-ava-duvernay-to-directing-blockbusters.html.

2. Connley, "How a Career Change"; Rebecca Farley, "A Reminder from Ava DuVernay: You Can Pivot at Any Point in Life," *Refinery29*, March 8, 2018, https://www.refinery29.com/en-us/2018/03/193002/ava-duvernay-storm-reid-facebook-live.

3. "Alexandria Ocasio-Cortez on the Future of the Democratic Party," *The View*, June 29, 2018, https://abcnews.go.com/theview/video/alexandria-ocasio-cortez-future-democratic-party-56265183.

4. Sharon Choe, "What These 14 Powerhouses Did before They Became Famous," *Oprah Daily*, August 20, 2018, https://www.oprahdaily.com/life/work-money/g22775608/successful-career-change/?slide=2.

5. Joan Michelson, "When You Want to Change Careers—7 Tips from Women Who Have Done It," *Forbes*, May 31, 2019, https://www.forbes.com/sites/joanmichelson2/2019/05/31/when-you-want-to-change-careers-7-tips-from-women-who-have-done-it/?sh=29c1a2d11fe4.

6. Caroline Castrillon, "How to Master Fear When Making a Career Change," *Forbes*, May 17, 2020, https://www.forbes.com/sites/carolinecastrillon/2020/05/17/how-to-master-fear-when-making-a-career-change/?sh=5cc3bdd460d6.

7. Jim Carrey, commencement speech, Maharishi International University, May 30, 2014, https://www.youtube.com/watch?v=V80-gPkpH6M.

Chapter 8

1. Tara Mohr, *Playing Big: Find Your Voice, Your Vision and Make Things Happen* (New York: Random House Business Books, 2022).

2. Margie Warrell, "Take a Risk: The Odds Are Better Than You Think," *Forbes*, June 18, 2013, https://www.forbes.com/sites/margiewarrell/2013/06/18/take-a-risk-the-odds-are-better-than-you-think/?sh=4bfc1c4e45c2.

3. "The Greatest Risks They Ever Took," *Forbes*, January 21, 2010, https://www.forbes.com/2010/01/20/greatest-risk-they-took-entrepreneurs-management-risk.html?sh=592e2fd33b2b.

4. Jill Griffin, "To Have a Great Career, Be a Risk Taker," *Forbes*, April 27, 2018, https://www.forbes.com/sites/jillgriffin/2018/04/27/to-have-a-great-career-be-a-risk-taker/?sh=23409ea374a2.

5. Alexia Fernandez Campbell, "Considering a Big Change? Go for It, Says Evidence from 20,000 Coin Flips," *The Atlantic*, August 9, 2016, https://www.theatlantic.com/business/archive/2016/08/quitting-your-job-and-other-life-choices/495122/.

Chapter 9

1. Claire Shipman and Katty Kay, *Womenomics: Write Your Own Rules for Success* (New York: HarperCollins, 2009).

2. Katty Kay and Claire Shipman, "The Confidence Gap," *The Atlantic*, May 2014, https://www.theatlantic.com/magazine/archive/2014/05/the-confidence-gap/359815/.

3. Kay and Shipman, "The Confidence Gap."

4. Institute of Leadership and Management, "Ambition and Gender at Work," accessed November 23, 2022, https://www.institutelm.com/static/uploaded/6151ed78-0ad1-495d-960e0ae40413b572.pdf.

5. Linda Babcock and Sara Laschever, *Women Don't Ask: Negotiation and the Gender Divide* (Princeton, NJ: Princeton University Press, 2003).

6. Kay and Shipman, "The Confidence Gap."

7. Kay and Shipman, "The Confidence Gap."

8. Ruchika Tulshyan and Jodi-Ann Burey, "Stop Telling Women They Have Imposter Syndrome," *Harvard Business Review*, February 11, 2021, https://hbr.org/2021/02/stop-telling-women-they-have-imposter-syndrome.

9. "Daughters Provide as Much Elderly Parent Care as They Can, Sons Do as Little as Possible," *Science Daily*, https://www.sciencedaily.com/releases/2014/08/140819082912.htm.

10. Arlie Hochschild, *The Second Shift: Working Families and the Revolution at Home* (New York: Penguin Books, 2012).

11. Stewart Friedman, "High-Powered Women and Supportive Spouses: Who's in Charge, and of What?" *Knowledge at Wharton*, November 7, 2012, https://knowledge.wharton.upenn.edu/article/high-powered-women-and-supportive-spouses-whos-in-charge-and-of-what-2/.

12. Friedman, "High-Powered Women."

13. Seramount, "Single Women in the Workforce," August 2017, https://seramount.com/research/research-report-single-women-in-workforce.

14. Friedman, "High-Powered Women."

15. Claire Cain Miller, "The World 'Has Found a Way to Do This': The U.S. Lags on Paid Leave," *New York Times*, October 25, 2021, https://www.nytimes.com/2021/10/25/upshot/paid-leave-democrats.html; see also Child Care Aware, "The US and the High Price of Child Care: 2019," accessed November 23, 2022, https://www.childcareaware.org/our-issues/research/the-us-and-the-high-price-of-child-care-2019/.

16. Marshall Plan for Moms, "The Business Case for Child Care: How Parent-Focused Employee Value Propositions Help Companies Win the War for Talent," accessed November 23, 2022, https://marshallplanformoms.com/childcare-report/.

17. Marshall Plan for Moms, "The Business Case for Child Care."

18. Marshall Plan for Moms, "The Business Case for Child Care."

19. See the Marshall Plan for Moms homepage, at https://marshallplanformoms.com/ (accessed November 23, 2022).

20. Eve Rodsky, *Fair Play: A Game-Changing Solution for When You Have Too Much to Do (and More Life to Live)* (New York: G. P. Putnam's Sons, 2019).

21. Rachel Rodgers, *We Should All Be Millionaires: A Woman's Guide to Earning More, Building Wealth, and Gaining Economic Power* (New York: HarperCollins Leadership, 2021).

Chapter 10

1. Anna Tingley, "Ava DuVernay on Moving from PR to Filmmaking, Directing 'When They See Us,'" *Variety*, August 9, 2019, https://variety.com/2019/tv/features/ava-duvernay-when-they-see-us-2-1203295840/.

2. Young-Jin Kim, "Flour's Joanne Chang Bet on Her Passion: Now She's a Baking Superstar," NBC 10 Boston, March 27, 2019, https://www.nbcboston.com/news/local/flour-joanne-chang-boston-baking-superstar/66614/.

3. Janelle Nanos, "Joanne Chang Won't Rest until Everything Is Perfect," *Boston Globe*, November 24, 2015, https://www.bostonglobe.com/magazine/2015/11/24/joanne-chang-won-rest-until-everything-perfect/83gpTFTylz2lg0j7iys2SM/story.html; Stephanie S. Lee, "Boston Pastry Chef Joanne Chang Follows Her Sweet Tooth to 'Flour,'" *Mochi Magazine*, April 20, 2011, https://www.mochimag.com/lifestyle/career/boston-pastry-chef-joanne-chang-follows-her-sweet-tooth-to-flour/.

4. Nanos, "Joanne Chang Won't Rest."

5. Jenny Blake, *Pivot: The Only Move That Matters Is Your Next One* (New York: Portfolio/Penguin, 2016).

Notes

6. Jenny Blake, "Pivot: The Only Move That Matters Is Your Next One," Talks at Google, October 26, 2016, https://www.youtube.com/watch?v=dL7LBoGIHZM.

7. Bridget Thoreson, "Forget Ladders, Think of Your Career as a River," *Next Web*, October 15, 2021, https://thenextweb.com/news/career-river-syndication.

8. Gert Schreuder and Melinde Coetzee, *Careers: An Organisational Perspective*, 3rd ed. (Lansdowne, South Africa: Juta Academic, 2007), 67.

Chapter 11

1. Dana Kanze, Laura Huang, Mark A. Conley, and E. Tory Higgins, "Male and Female Entrepreneurs Get Asked Different Questions by VCs—and It Affects How Much Funding They Get," *Harvard Business Review*, June 27, 2017, https://hbr.org/2017/06/male-and-female-entrepreneurs-get-asked-different-questions-by-vcs-and-it-affects-how-much-funding-they-get.

2. Elana Lyn Gross, "How to Close the Venture Capital Gender Gap Faster," *Forbes*, May 20, 2019, https://www.forbes.com/sites/elanagross/2019/05/20/venture-capital-gender-gap/?sh=3f83886d7a58.

3. Alisha Haridasani Gupta, "Funding for Start-Ups Founded by Women Is Surging," *New York Times*, November 2, 2021, https://www.nytimes.com/2021/11/02/business/dealbook/female-founded-startups-vc-funding.html; "The Venture Capital World Has a Problem with Women of Color," *Girlboss*, accessed November 23, 2022, https://girlboss.com/blogs/read/venture-capital-woc-women-of-color.

4. Morgan Stanley, "The Growing Market Investors Are Missing," 2018, https://www.morganstanley.com/content/dam/msdotcom/mcil/growing-market-investors-are-missing.pdf.

5. Kamal Hassan, Monisha Varadan, and Claudia Zeisberger, "How the VC Pitch Process Is Failing Female Entrepreneurs," *Harvard Business Review*, January 13, 2020, https://hbr.org/2020/01/how-the-vc-pitch-process-is-failing-female-entrepreneurs.

6. Hassan, Varadan, and Zeisberger, "How the VC Pitch Process"; Kanze et al., "Male and Female Entrepreneurs."

7. Alexander W. Watts, "Why Does John Get the STEM Job Rather than Jennifer?" Stanford University, June 2, 2014, https://gender.stanford.edu/news-publications/gender-news/why-does-john-get-stem-job-rather-jennifer.

8. Molly Savard, "Kim Malek's Sweet Success," *Shondaland*, July 30, 2018, https://www.shondaland.com/live/a22823535/kim-maleks-salt-and-straw-ice-cream-interview/.

Chapter 12

1. "Tina Fey's Aha! Moment," *O*, June 2003, https://www.oprah.com/spirit/tina-feys-aha-moment.
2. "Tina Fey's Aha! Moment"; see also Christobel Hastings, "Careers Advice: 12 Remarkable Women on the Career Moments That Changed Their Lives," *Stylist*, accessed May 4, 2022, https://www.stylist.co.uk/long-reads/careers-advice-from-successful-women-how-they-made-it-changing-career-success-money/351255.
3. Reshma Saujani, *Brave, Not Perfect: Fear Less, Fail More, and Live Bolder* (New York: Currency, 2019).
4. Saujani, *Brave, Not Perfect*.
5. Saujani, *Brave, Not Perfect*.
6. Saujani, *Brave, Not Perfect*.
7. Adrian Granzella Larsson, "7 Successful Women on the 'Mistakes' That Changed Their Careers," *Fast Company*, September 20, 2019, https://www.fastcompany.com/90406108/7-successful-women-on-the-mistakes-that-changed-their-careers.
8. "21 Inspiring Career Quotes from Women Who Changed the Game," *Girlboss*, accessed May 4, 2022, https://girlboss.com/blogs/read/best-career-quotes-from-women.

Chapter 13

1. McKinsey and Company, "Women in the Workplace, 2022," October 18, 2022, https://www.mckinsey.com/featured-insights/diversity-and-inclusion/women-in-the-workplace.
2. Julie Ma and Brooke LaMantia, "It's Never Too Late: 25 Famous Women on Starting Over in a New Career," *The Cut*, March 21, 2002, https://www.thecut.com/article/famous-women-on-switching-careers.html.
3. Mike Oppland, "8 Ways to Create Flow According to Mihaly Csikszentmihalyi," *Positive Psychology*, August 12, 2021, https://positivepsychology.com/mihaly-csikszentmihalyi-father-of-flow/.
4. Steven Kotler, "The Science of Peak Human Performance," *Time*, April 30, 2014, https://time.com/56809/the-science-of-peak-human-performance/.
5. Kotler, "The Science of Peak Human Performance."
6. Kotler, "The Science of Peak Human Performance."
7. Kotler, "The Science of Peak Human Performance."

Chapter 14

1. Caroline Castrillon, "Why More Women Are Turning to Entrepreneurship," *Forbes*, February 4, 2019, https://www.forbes.com/sites/carolinecastrillon/2019/02/04/why-more-women-are-turning-to-entrepreneurship/?sh=39e3081542a7; McKinsey and Company, "Women in the Workplace, 2019," 2019, https://wiw-report.s3.amazonaws.com/Women_in_the_Workplace_2019.pdf.

2. Castrillon, "Why More Women Are Turning to Entrepreneurship"; Stephen Turban, Laura Freeman, and Ben Waber, "A Study Used Sensors to Show That Men and Women Are Treated Differently at Work," *Harvard Business Review*, October 23, 2017, https://hbr.org/2017/10/a-study-used-sensors-to-show-that-men-and-women-are-treated-differently-at-work.

3. Zuhairah Washington and Laura Morgan Roberts, "Women of Color Get Less Support at Work: Here's How Managers Can Change That," *Harvard Business Review*, March 4, 2019, https://hbr.org/2019/03/women-of-color-get-less-support-at-work-heres-how-managers-can-change-that; Nielsen, "African-American Women: Our Science, Her Magic," September 21, 2017, https://www.nielsen.com/us/en/insights/report/2017/african-american-women-our-science-her-magic.

4. McKinsey and Company and Lean In, "Women in the Workplace, 2021," 2021, https://www.mckinsey.com/~/media/mckinsey/featured%20insights/diversity%20and%20inclusion/women%20in%20the%20workplace%202021/women-in-the-workplace-2021.pdf.

5. Washington and Roberts, "Women of Color Get Less Support."

6. Lean In, "The State of Black Women in Corporate America," accessed May 4, 2022, https://media.sgff.io/sgff_r1eHetbDYb/2020-08-13/1597343917539/Lean_In_-_State_of_Black_Women_in_Corporate_America_Report_1.pdf.

7. Ria Bhagwat, "More Women Are Becoming Entrepreneurs than Ever," *Good Good Good*, November 9, 2021, https://www.goodgoodgood.co/articles/more-women-are-becoming-entrepreneurs-than-ever.

8. Donna Kelley, Mahdi Majbouri, and Angela Randolph, "Black Women Are More Likely to Start a Business than White Men," *Harvard Business Review*, May 11, 2021, https://hbr.org/2021/05/black-women-are-more-likely-to-start-a-business-than-white-men.

Chapter 15

1. Jenny Blake, *Pivot: The Only Move That Matters Is Your Next One* (New York: Portfolio/Penguin, 2016), 4.

2. Robert H. Waterman Jr., Judith A. Waterman, Betsy A. Collard, "Toward a Career-Resilient Workforce," *Harvard Business Review*, July–August 1994, https://hbr.org/1994/07/toward-a-career-resilient-workforce.

3. Gert Schreuder and Melinde Coetzee, *Careers: An Organisational Perspective*, 3rd ed. (Lansdowne, South Africa: Juta Academic, 2007).

4. Caroline Castrillon, "Why Resilience Can Make or Break Your Career," *Forbes*, October 13, 2019, https://www.forbes.com/sites/carolinecastrillon/2019/10/13/why-resilience-can-make-or-break-your-career/?sh=3ada645018e6.

Conclusion

1. Bridget Thoreson, "Busting the Career Ladder Myth," Zapier, October 4, 2021, https://zapier.com/blog/career-river/.

ABOUT THE AUTHOR

JESSICA GALICA has built an accomplished and unique business career spanning almost every kind of corporate work environment, including management consulting at the prestigious Bain & Company and work at industry giants like Apple, Siemens, and various start-ups. In 2020 she began researching and writing about women's experiences in the workplace.

Jess's career shift was driven by her transformative journey stepping into motherhood. When she had her first child, she craved a more authentic and purposeful career. Through initial research she quickly discovered that her story—building a stellar career, doing everything "right," but waking up lost—is not unique. Today, drawing from her personal story and armed with insights from studying the career trajectories of more than 150 highly successful women, Jess has emerged as a leading authority on women's career reinvention. As a business leader, an executive coach for high-performing women, and a charismatic corporate speaker and podcast host, she engages with experts and professional women on topics such as how to build meaningful careers, advocate for workplace equity, and navigate the delicate balance between motherhood and professional ambitions.

Jess holds an MBA from MIT's Sloan School of Management, where she received double scholarships, and a BA from Georgetown University. Importantly, Jess treasures her role as a present mom to her two kids.